AVALON

BY VANESSA MORGAN

Cover design by Gilles Vranckx.

AUTHOR'S NOTE

Everything in this book is true to my memory of it. In some instances, time was compressed or altered slightly to facilitate an economical telling of the story. I had to leave a lot out.

ALSO BY VANESSA MORGAN

NOVELS

Drowned Sorrow

SHORT STORIES

The Strangers Outside

SCREENPLAYS

A Good Man

GPS with Benefits

Next to Her

Special thanks to

Gilles Vranckx and Anne Billson

"Everything terrible is something that needs our love."

— Rainer Maria Rilke

"When we have the deepest affection for an animal, we do not possess that love but are possessed by it."

— Dean R. Koontz

THE NEW KID ON THE BLOCK

The first time I met Avalon was on March 16, 2001.

It was well past midnight. As my boyfriend, Stephan, and I drove home south across Brussels, people crowded the pavements; most were coming or going or chattering in front of a bar. The lights blazed bright in the mid-March night sky. Belgium showed the first signs of spring, and the temperature was surprisingly mild, even at night.

We had spent the evening at the Brussels International Fantastic Film Festival, which was one of my happy places. I had been hosting Q&As there since college and it was there that I met Stephan four years earlier.

By the time we arrived in our hometown, Oudergem, a mostly elderly neighborhood in the outskirts of the Belgian capital, Brussels, the streets had cleared. There wasn't a single person in sight. We drove along the street perpendicular to ours, when an oversized white cat with ginger patches crossed right in front of us. Piercing green eyes lit up his striking features.

"That's the Turkish Van cat I told you about," Stephan said.

We'd been obsessed with the breed for years. Once, on the Greek island of Lesbos, Stephan had adopted a Van kitten, and though the cat had stayed with his ex-girlfriend, he had a soft spot for the breed and had infected me with that obsession. After looking at countless photos on the Internet, we were adamant to adopt one of our own. To our disappointment, there were no Turkish Van cat breeders in Belgium, and even visits to cat shows turned out fruitless. So instead we saved a Van-patterned moggy from a shelter and pretended he was the Turkish Van we'd been searching for. This type of cat was so rare in Belgium that there was absolutely no chance to see one roaming about. Yet over the past few days, Stephan had told me he'd spotted one in our neighborhood.

And now that cat stood right in front of us.

As soon as we parked the car and got out, the Turkish Van cat stopped in his tracks and sized me up as if he recognized me. Then he came over to greet us.

I couldn't resist kneeling down and stroking him, partly to make friends and partly to see if this gorgeous creature wore any form of identification. I was curious to know more about him.

"He's not wearing a collar," I said.

"I think he's lost. The supermarket where I've seen him earlier this week is way too far for his territory."

The supermarket was far indeed. But then again, cats could sometimes roam over great distances. I once read about a feral cat whose range covered 1,351 acres or 2.1 square miles.

So what were the possibilities? A cat of this rare species couldn't possibly be a stray. I didn't believe he was lost either. He was too thickset and clean, his eyes too clear, and his fur too soft. He probably just lost his collar along the way. In the worst-case scenario, he was an indoor cat that got out by accident and couldn't find his way home.

"Maybe he hasn't eaten for days. I'll go fetch him something, just in case," Stephan said.

A few minutes later, he was back with a small plate of canned food, which the cat finished in a matter of seconds.

I picked up the empty plate, and gave him a ruffle before heading home.

As soon as we moved, he followed us.

At the front door, we fobbed him off with a gentle nudge, but the cat forced his way in. We pushed a little harder; he did too. So it went for several minutes, but there was no way this feline would remain outside. It was evident he wanted to stay the night.. Whether our two cats and guinea pig would agree, was another issue. Not that they had any say in it. Our new feline guest had already made the decision for us.

We put the new cat in our office, which was connected to our bedroom and separated by a sliding glass door, and we provided him with a clean litter box made out of cardboard and newspapers, a bowl of food, and fresh water.

Our cats, Ballon and Tigris, immediately detected the intruder. They planted themselves in front of the sliding glass door and watched the newcomer while spitting out little mews that sounded like questions: *Who is this cat? Where does he come from?*

"We'd better be on the look-out for missing cat announcements in the area tomorrow," I said. "If he's really lost, someone might go looking for him."

Sitting on my bed, I took one last look at this stunning creature before I turned out the lights for the night.

.

DR. HENRI

Cats are renowned for being tense and apprehensive in a new habitat, and many of them hide and refuse to eat. This new cat was the opposite. He couldn't be more comfortable. Not a single noise had come from him during the night, and now he sat in a relaxed pose in our office, waiting serenely for destiny to unfold.

Our ways would part after today. With two cats and a guinea pig, we were already looking like pet hoarders. We couldn't possibly add a new cat to the collection, no matter how much we had dreamed about this breed. But as I sat on my bed, watching him from behind the sliding glass door, I had the odd feeling that this cat belonged here somehow.

I opened the door to invite the new cat into the bedroom. He immediately sauntered in my direction, allowing me to pet his downy coat while he quietly purred away.

"Making friends, huh?" Stephan said as he entered. He sat down next to me, and we both bore witness to this feline's refined tenderness and fragility. As if he were an expensive brittle object from a box that read, "Handle with care," this cat inspired delicacy and respect.

"So what do we do now?" I asked.

"Why don't we keep him a couple of days, the time we need to pin down his owners?"

"I don't think that's such a good idea."

"Why not? Ballon and Tigris seem to be at ease with his presence."

"I have the feeling he belongs to me already and he's only been here for one night. I'm afraid that I'd want to keep him if he stays with us," I said. "We can drop him off at Dr. Henri. What do you think?"

Dr. Henri was our pets' veterinarian. Three years ago, when a tiny tabby of only a few weeks old jumped into my boyfriend's arms as he exited the supermarket, Dr. Henri agreed to keep her in custody for a while. Instead of locking the kitten up in a cage, she stayed in his living room and played with his children. After a week, we decided on adopting the tabby and called her Tigris.

Stephan agreed that Dr. Henri was the best option, so that's exactly who we went to. He gladly offered us the help we needed.

For the following days, we distributed flyers to the nearby shops, restaurants, and supermarkets, and we phoned every shelter and veterinarian in the area to check for missing cats.

After two weeks had passed, no one had claimed the cat. Dr. Henri called us to say he needed to make space for new animals.

"Your stray is quite the character," he said as we arrived on March 30.

"What do you mean?"

"He craves attention. A *lot* of attention."

His spouse entered, holding the cat.

"Here we are: our little devil," Dr. Henri said.

His spouse smiled unevenly at his remark. She put him onto the examination table where he immediately walked up to me.

"There are two choices," Dr. Henri explained. "Either you take him to a shelter, or you adopt this cat yourselves."

The first option was out of the question. Four years before, we adopted our first cat, Ballon, in a shelter. The office where we signed the adoption papers was filled with a dozen dustbins, all of them filled to the brim with euthanized cats. I wasn't aware at that time that there was such a thing as no-kill shelters, so I refused this new cat the possible horrors of an early death.

That left us with option number two: adopting him.

"The only thing I'm worried about is the health of my own cats," Stephan said. "Are they at risk of getting sick because of this one?"

"I've already examined him and he's in good shape. There's no problem for your other cats."

"How old is he?" I asked.

"I'd say he's about one and a half."

"I'm ready to take him home," I said.

"If he's about to become a regular here, I'll have to create a file for him. Have you decided on a name yet?"

I immediately thought about the Mamoru Oshii movie *Avalon* we watched at the festival on the night this cat followed us home. It was a visually pleasing Japanese/Polish action-drama in which a geeky girl spends her days either cooking for her dog or escaping the real world by playing a futuristic battle simulation game.

"Avalon," I said without hesitation. "His name's Avalon."

Doctor Henri smiled. "Be good to your new owner, Avalon."

He had no idea.

I BELONG TO YOU, AND YOU BELONG TO ME

Before taking Avalon home, Stephan and I discussed the best way to introduce him to his new environment. Our resolution was that he should be confined to our office for a few days. We felt he was more likely to grow comfortable and familiar with his surroundings and our other pets if he wasn't intimidated by too much change at once. Ballon and Tigris had been introduced to their new home one room at a time over a period of several days, and that worked out fine.

We didn't worry about Ballon and Tigris' reactions to the newcomer. Both were social and patient.

Carrying Avalon in a light-gray cat carrier, I crossed the front door to our apartment. Avalon didn't make any sound, but he balled himself up in the corner of his carrier as Ballon and Tigris approached to sniff at it. Ballon peered with interest at the carrier's contents, but Tigris took one whiff and backed up several feet.

"You guys can play later," I told them and headed to my home office, closing the door behind me. I set the carrier down and unlatched it, lifting Avalon out. He seemed confused, but after a couple of minutes he emptied the food bowl that we had set up.

Ballon and Tigris were observing us from the other side of the sliding glass door. I liked that they could see the new arrival at all times, but physical contact had to wait until the cats were more comfortable in each other's presence.

Over the next few days, Avalon received more space to acquaint himself with his new home. After such a session, Avalon returned to his office while Ballon and Tigris could explore his scents.

After about a week, I felt that it was time for the cats to meet in person.

Upon being released from his confinement, Avalon went straight to the kitchen toward Ballon's and Tigris' food dishes. The other cats circled him cautiously. Ballon was the first to hiss, then Tigris. Avalon couldn't care less. It seemed as if Ballon and Tigris hissed to thin air. Without looking up, Avalon finished the food in a matter of mere seconds. Stomach full, he went about exploring the apartment, the others trailing his steps.

I tried not to pay them too much attention to avoid excess stress, so I went about my daily activities. With my laptop, I settled in the sofa to work on a story, and Tigris followed suit, positioning herself next to me, her body touching mine.

As soon as Avalon noticed her, he stopped in his tracks, a hurt expression shimmering in his eyes.

I put my laptop aside and tapped on the space next to me to urge Avalon to join us. Instead of coming over, he just stood there. He looked so defeated, I pitied him. I called his name again, but he didn't budge. After I tried once more, he finally did a few cautious steps forward and jumped onto my lap.

Tigris lifted her head, sniffing him inquisitively. Avalon's paw came up in immediate response. With slitted eyelids, he pushed Tigris to the ground. She looked up, bewildered. Her face read, *What is going on here?* She and Ballon often slept together on my lap, so this was a new situation.

In an effort to put up a defense against Avalon, Tigris approached me again, but one single tap from Avalon, whose body weight easily matched our other two cats put together, immediately brought her back to where she came from.

Like a possessive husband who puts his arm around his wife in public as a mark of ownership, Avalon took possession of me. And just like that jealous husband, Avalon eyed his surroundings to make sure no one even looked at his love interest.

And that was just the beginning of it.

***

One of the main characteristics of Turkish Van cats is the way they regard love: "I belong to you, and you belong to me." This was absolutely true in Avalon's case.

If another pet was curled up on my chest, he batted angrily at their heads. Ballon, who was the gentlest cat of all, regarded himself as too mature not to have to submit to Avalon's kingship but Tigris found herself crowded out. Whenever Avalon spotted her in my proximity, her life was in danger. Avalon leapt onto Tigris, sinking teeth and claws into her neck, and crushing her spine. He never backed away in confused alarm if she squealed in pain, so his intention was definitely to hurt her.

Avalon not only wanted exclusivity, he also wanted *constant* attention. He needed to sit with me, or on me, at all times. If Avalon's need for love wasn't met, he wandered around the apartment at loose ends, "complaining" at the top of his lungs, or working out his frustration on our furniture or whatever was in his immediate proximity. He clawed the wallpaper to shreds as his fancy dictated, and scaled our bookcases so he could throw mounds of DVDs onto the floor to bat around. I can't tell you how many times I came home to find a ransacked apartment that looked like a crime scene – a cyclone of bare DVDs and shredded boxes strewn across the hallway.

His love was intense, overwhelming, and didn't allow any other cat or person in my life. Even though I did my utmost to show how utterly smitten I was, his eyes were perpetually covered with a dark veil of frustration. Even during lap time, he kept a half eye on his surroundings, his muscles stiff as piecrust.

I wondered what had made Avalon this way--if it was indeed just part of the breed's characteristics, or if he had brought scars with him from his kittenhood. Because he held himself in a way that oozed superiority, others assured me he was a pretentious miscreant. I couldn't blame them. Avalon behaved as if he was the chosen one. Everything and everyone belonged to him, and with his aggressive character and impressive ten kilos, no one dared to say otherwise.

I refused to believe that this was all there was to this cat.

Doing research on his type of personality, I learned that a cat that tries to hog all our love usually had to endure heartbreak or deprivation in the past. He holds the false belief that caring is in short supply; if we give a slice of warmth to another, it is taken from him. As the cat fears the loss of love, he demands what he sees as a limited resource, so he displays anger and aggression when his person shows affection towards others.

But knowing the reasons behind his behavior didn't make life with Avalon any easier.

AVALON

Dr. Henri advised us not to indulge Avalon's demands, and to give every cat its fair share of lap-time. Avalon quickly turned from bad to worse. Resentment made way for downright violence. I spent long hours training Avalon to respect Ballon and Tigris, issuing a harsh, "No," and ending the battle when it became too violent.

It was of no use.

In his attempts to be loved, Avalon quickly found himself despised by everyone but me.

All I wanted was to show this cat how crazy I was about him, but no matter what I did, nothing enabled him to crawl out of the dark hole he had dug for himself.

AL CAPONE THE CAT

On a hot night in mid-May I startled awake at four o'clock in the morning to the screeching sound of what seemed like an oriental small-clawed otter begging for food. My first thought was, *One of my cats is hurt*, and I scrambled in the dark toward the noise.

Faint light streamed in through the blinds from the streetlights outside. Avalon squared off against the sliding glass door toward the garden, puffed up to twice his normal size. He arched his back, and every hair on his body stood up straight. His tail bristled, stiff as a broomstick. Although he tucked his head down low, his ears rose to full attention. With legs set wide apart, he extended his front claws farther than I'd ever seen them, farther than I would have thought physically possible. His devilish growl rose drastically in both volume and pitch. I've heard angry cats hiss and bristle before, but in Avalon's case it seemed to be a demonic possession.

The reason for all this dramatic behavior was another cat passing through our garden. An exquisite creature, he was almost as big as Avalon, sporting a dark-gray coat with a purple undertone, and big orange eyes. The intruder didn't growl or hiss or puff. He just stood there, looking inside.

Avalon cried so loud that the cat on the other side of the window tried to shore up his defenses and held the line for about ten seconds before backing away and leaving in anxious disgust.

I kneeled down next to Avalon and stroked his fur in an attempt to calm him down. The staccato pounding of his heart alarmed me, as was the heavy panting, and the expanding and shrinking of his rib cage in rapid succession. He could literally die of heartbreak.

Avalon's streaks of jealousy inside the house were already notorious, and it didn't take long before the neighbors' cats knew about his temper. Avalon was the Al Capone of Brussels. The most feared criminal in the neighborhood was a snarling, furious, out-of-control feline. Most cats never skulked around our garden ever again. The ones that did, regretted it soon afterwards.

But it would be unjust to say that Avalon treated all cats equally. True, he didn't like any creature, but some of them were definitely more hated than others. For some reason Avalon always knew-- *knew* --when I thought a cat was handsome. As soon as I started thinking, *This one isn't too bad looking*, his jealousy surfaced. Avalon galvanized into action, propelled himself toward the window, growling like a ferocious animal, and thrust the whole weight of his body forward, smashing himself against the window with a loud hiss that bared his fangs. And if that didn't work, Avalon let go with a stream of urine.

No one messed with Al Capone the cat.

But he wasn't as violent if I thought the intruding cat was average looking. He was on his guard, but that was it. Avalon picked up on my feelings somehow. It was eerie how much he actually knew.

AVALON

One day, I scooped Avalon up during one of his jealous streaks with a neighbor's cat, kissed his ferocious little head, and quietly told him that he shouldn't care about other cats because he was the only one that mattered to me, those other felines were nothing compared to him, and I was utterly smitten with my soul cat. He may not have understood the words, but he figured out what I was telling him. Avalon's breathing and heartbeat slowed, and he licked my face as if to say, *Thank you for choosing me over him.*

But something changed in me as well. I'd known since day one that I was madly in love with Avalon, but as I expressed my feelings, I could sense the truth and depth of those words like never before.

From then on, out of respect for Avalon, I never again paid attention to other cats. Sure, I noticed them, but no feelings were ever involved.

It was exactly what Avalon needed. Whenever another feline encroached on his territory, he calmed down as soon as he felt my love for him. After a short while, Avalon didn't care about other cats anymore and he just went about his day, whether there were other felines around or not.

Avalon's demands were simple. He wanted exclusivity. But isn't that what we all want? Avalon was only being more expressive and neurotic about it. He needed to be assured that I loved only him.

Al Capone the cat had a tender heart, after all.

KINDRED SPIRITS

I often reflected upon why I felt so protective about Avalon. The answer was because I understood him. Though it took me years to acknowledge, Avalon and I were kindred spirits; his insecurities and need for love echoed my own.

I may be fortunate to make a living as a writer and travel the world as part of my job these days, but this was not always the case. It's embarrassing sometimes to open up about my past, because we live in a world where struggle is frowned upon. However, when Avalon and I met, we were two broken beings trying to find our place in the world, and not succeeding.

It started-- as is usually the case in such situations-- in my childhood.

After my parents' divorce, when I was six or seven years old, my mother sat down next to me on my bed.

"I have cancer," she announced. "Do you know what that means?"

I shook my head.

"That means I am sick and I'm going to die."

It was the first time I was confronted with the finiteness of life. That night, I cried incessantly.

My mother didn't die, though. She didn't die because there was no cancer.

What she did have was a need for attention, and announcing to a six-year-old that you are going to die turned out to be extremely effective.

Once the believability of the cancer story became dubious due to a lack of treatments and symptoms, there was a complete list of other illnesses to go through-- malaria, brucellosis, celiac disease-- the list got so long it was difficult to keep up with it. She probably did get some of those, but once she started lying, no one could distinguish the lie from the truth anymore.

Years later, I often found her asleep on the toilet, with a near empty bottle of whiskey on her lap. She hid those bottles in a box near the toilet bowl. Others were safely tucked away in the back of her wardrobe. I informed her parents about this, but the confrontation led to even more drinking. In the end, the abuse of alcohol materialized real illnesses. At least she didn't have to pretend anymore.

When I was seventeen years old, a truck hit me as I exit school. I was on my way to my grandparents for lunch. Because I was homebound with concussion and severe pains for several weeks, friends visited daily and stayed the evening to keep me company and to watch horror videos.

My mother told me, "By the time you recover from the accident, your friends will be my friends and they won't be paying attention to you anymore."

She succeeded.

For those who didn't visit me at home, she had other plans. One evening she phoned my classmates and lied about me.

The following day, my schoolmates either ignored or insulted me.

"Why are you all behaving this way?" I asked.

"Because you're backstabbing us and jealous," one student said.

"Excuse me?"

"Your mother called us yesterday to warn us about you."

"She lied. I'm not like that."

"Then how come she called us?"

"I don't know. To hurt me, maybe."

"Mothers don't hurt their children. Mothers don't lie."

They were right. They don't. And I couldn't understand why mine did.

Her acts taught me that what I had could easily be taken away. Even though other people lied to get what they wanted, I didn't. So I considered myself a victim, someone whose path to happiness would be strenuous.

My father awoke in me a different set of insecurities.

I had the impression I wasn't the daughter he wished he'd had, and his demand for perfection mingled with authority and a firm hand. Whenever I was unable to accomplish something, say an algebra puzzle, his frustration expressed itself through physical and verbal brutality.

Not only did my father want perfection and compliance, he also often reminded me that I was too mediocre for what I wanted. When I told him as a child that I wanted to grow up to become a model, he asked me if I had taken a good look at myself. When I wanted to get a university degree and become a journalist, he said I was too stupid. And when I wanted to write a book, he said no one apart from a few friends would ever read it.

One day I asked him why he was so negative. He replied, "I'm not going to tell you you're doing something good just because you're my daughter." I had to earn my compliments.

I remember him stating once that he didn't want me to grow up pretentious. Mission accomplished. Whenever I looked into the mirror, I saw someone ugly. Whenever I looked at my work, I saw a lack of talent and intelligence.

I proved him wrong on many occasions. I got my university degree. I became a writer. I sold many books.

It was never enough. When I published my first novel, he told me my one-book-resume looked ridiculous compared to bibliographies from authors with over ten books. When I came back to Belgium from having lived a year in London, he forced me to admit that I had failed, even though I was just bored of London and wanted to start writing instead of working in theatre.

After reading a first draft of this book, my sister told me that my father often says how proud he is of my degree and my books. Hearing those words touched me. He didn't even need to be proud; I just wanted to be loved the way I loved him.

Classmates, too, let me know at every occasion how uncool and awkward I was. Even teachers made fun of me. I didn't have many friends, and those I had often led me to believe I was inferior to them. When I talked, no one listened.

My grandparents on my mother's side were the only ones who showed me love through both words and actions, and who expressed their opinions without criticizing.

My parents must have loved me in their own way, I suppose. At least, that's what I'd like to believe. I'm sure they had brought me up to the best of their abilities, but I couldn't shake off the feeling that I disappointed my father, and that my mother was too busy looking for attention to be able to give some to me.

As a result, I forced myself into silence, a subconscious reaction to protect myself against negativity. It also instilled in me a deep-grounded fear for imperfection and failure. I thought I needed to be flawless in order to be loved, so I shut myself off from people, especially those I estimated highly.

Books and movies were the only place where I could hide from my insecurities. As a child, I read anything I could get my hands on. I started with popular authors such as Stephen King and Agatha Christie, went on to read my way through all the English, American, and French classics, and ended up discovering Nietzsche, Shakespeare, Proust and Brecht, while others my age were still reading *The Smurfs*. At my father's, where everything was put into question, I read at night, under the covers, with only a pillow light to provide enough illumination to distinguish the words. At my mother's, I could read suicide guides without her raising an eyebrow. Movies were reserved for the exam period. I passed my exams in the morning, rented a couple of videos on my way back home, and spent the rest of the afternoon watching films that were too advanced for my age.

When I wasn't emerging myself in stories, I pulled myself back in daydreams. In those fantasies, I saw myself at my highest and believed that this was what I would one day become. I thought this through in such a detailed manner I could smell, taste, and feel the future. I never wondered how life would turn out, because I just knew. I recognized there would be hardships along the way, but if I worked hard at eliminating my flaws everything would turn out fine.

***

As I grew older, I didn't want others' predictions and opinions to be more important than my own. That's why I took matters into my own hands. I started to make life happen for myself. Like many young adults have experienced, though, my path to success wasn't a straight one. After four successful years at the university, I moved to London for a year to volunteer in theatre. When I returned to Belgium I worked for several magazines as a freelance journalist. Two years later, the majority of those magazines had gone bankrupt and I found myself in a new freelance teaching job that I hated. There wasn't anything wrong with the job-- many colleagues loved it--but a shy girl like myself felt ill at ease in front of large groups.

I once read, "If you don't like something about your life, change it," so that's what I tried to do.

While living in London, I had developed the desire to write fiction after seeing a theatre performance of William Faulkner's *As I Lay Dying*. I took my frustration with the new job as an opportunity to work on my dream of being a writer, and I spent every free hour setting goals, writing stories, editing, and looking for solutions.

Obviously, writing books wasn't that easy. I had put the bar unrealistically high, and ignored the long learning curve. By trying to go beyond my limits, I was defining them. I wanted to create beauty, but conceived only plainness. I feared that any writing talent I had was an illusion.

Just as obviously, not everything went according to plan. I had started teaching halftime to be able to write more, but the government found my drop of income suspicious, and doubled my taxes and added a fine, with the result that I had to teach even more than before. A film production company promised me a screenwriting contract, then disappeared from the planet. And when I wanted to self-publish a book after months searching for the ideal company, the publisher took the money but never printed it.

I needed Stephan to support me with this, to be the first person to say, "I know you can do this. I believe in you." However, though he was supportive, he wasn't a dreamer at all, and didn't believe a girl without connections would be able to sell any stories.

Meanwhile, I searched for another job, something easy that would take the pressure off. I was tired of struggling and hoping. Again my efforts were getting me nowhere. I tried working in a video store and doing administrative work, but for everything I wanted to do, I was overqualified.

All of these were setbacks that many people in their twenties faced, but it felt as if someone told me, "Don't even try. You are not meant to be happy." In everything I did, even if it was just playing a board game, I saw proof that I was born unlucky. It was a crazy idea, yet I believed it wholeheartedly.

My writing reflected that line of thinking. My characters fought hard for what they wanted, but in the end, they never got it. I had come to believe it was the way life worked; there would be no happy ending.

Yet I never gave up--*Keep going. Keep moving forward, and things will get better.* I needed to tell myself that there was this light at the end of the tunnel. Deep down, I had ceased to believe the light existed, but if it did, I didn't want to miss it by not walking in that direction.

In *The Strangers Outside*, a short story I wrote several years later, the main character says, "Passive people fail. For the others there's at least a chance." I'd only just come to understand the importance of that phrase in my life. Until then, I had unconsciously lived by that quote. Although I didn't believe in a happy ending, I didn't give up.

But I also wondered, when was the expiration date to realizing one's dreams? I had once read that the moment you give up is the precise moment you would have succeeded. But was that true? I knew artists who had reached retirement age, but who still struggled to even start their career. Would I be one of them someday? Was I maybe not good enough for what I wanted? People had been telling me this all my life. Maybe I'd better believe them and stop fighting against it. But how could I be sure?

As the years passed with nothing to show for my efforts, my frustration grew into full-blown desperation. When you're young, life and time seem endless, but as you get older you get more desperate. All I wanted was to be a good person and to find contentment in a job. I didn't understand how that could be so difficult. I wasn't striving for fame and riches. I just wanted to be happy.

I was afraid that family and friends would abandon me if they'd found out what a failure I was. Some already had. I stopped seeing them altogether--only until I was progressing, or so I told myself. If a friend called, I didn't pick up the phone.

At work, people didn't notice what was going on, because I practiced my professional smile to perfection.

"It's so obvious that you were born to teach, that you're doing this job with all your heart," my students often said.

"Thank you," I replied with a smile.

Inside, though, I was crying.

No one knew about my alternate inner life. I behaved like a schizophrenic, except that I could distinguish between fantasy and reality. The real girl was the one from my imagination; the other one was who I was forced to be.

My pets were the only ones who anaesthetized that hopelessness. When I believed that nothing would ever work out for me, they still made me smile. When I thought that I was unworthy of being loved, they showed me they cared. And then there was Avalon, who, because of his own traumas and imperfections, made me feel understood. So when I lay awake at night, going over how unlucky I was, and Avalon slid next to me to fall asleep in my arms, I thought, "I am so lucky to have found you."

THEFT

Psychoanalysts claim that we spend our adult lives healing childhood traumas. Personally, I was healing the scars of unworthiness, lies, and dominance. I wanted to express my thoughts in books since I didn't have the courage to express them in reality, to look for professional freedom whereas I only needed to be free from my past, and to have meaningful relationships with my cats because I was unable to relate to human beings.

I wondered in what measure Avalon was trying to heal *his* childhood traumas. Considering the effort he put into it, there must have been a lot to deal with.

As many others couldn't relate to the same issues, they didn't look beyond Avalon's violent and selfish behavior. They couldn't see the hidden soft spot that yearned for love. And so Avalon swelled disfavor within everyone. Friends and family members who had initially admired his breathtaking handsomeness, quickly turned their backs on him, rolling their eyes at his unmannerliness. Therefore I fell into disfavor as well. Not only did I have the unforgivable idea to keep such a villain, but I adored and defended him as well.

Riled by his behavior, our landlord started a vendetta against him. In her forties and heavily afflicted by Multiple Sclerosis, she swore by eliminating all nasty things from her life, Avalon included.

"I warned you. Only pets are allowed in this apartment. No other animals," she said.

"But Avalon *is* a pet."

The landlord looked at Avalon as if he was something unpalatable. "That thing is the spawn of Satan."

"I know he can be a bit of a pain sometimes, but he's just a cat."

In the background, making the guttural noise of a lion devouring its prey, Avalon held Tigris in a death grip, trying to bite her head off. When Tigris escaped, Avalon ran past us like a whirlwind, growling, flew into a full skid, crashed into the coffee table, went airborne, crawled on the casing of the living room door, right up to the ceiling, jumped off, and collided head-on with our landlord who jumped in mortal fear.

"Either you throw that *beast* out or I'll throw *you* out," she hissed.

***

Thinking about the possible reasons why Avalon had been on the street, I imagined his humans thinking, *We can't handle him anymore.* Avalon might have been an absolute traffic-stopper in terms of beauty, but my guess was that when his owners noticed how boisterous, dominant, frisky, and mental he was, they took him for a ride and threw him out on to the roadside.

Another possibility was that he got out by accident and that his owners thought, *Phew. We finally got rid of him. Let's just keep the doors and windows shut, so he can't get in.*

A pet psychic once told me that she sensed two brothers had been cocky with Avalon. "He ran away; he couldn't put up with their attitude," she said. "A woman was kind to him, but whenever she wasn't looking, the two boys abused him. Avalon was only about nine days on the streets when you found and rescued him. You were his angel. This had to happen."

Of course, this may not have been the case, especially because other things she said turned out to be incorrect. However, it was the only information I got, so that's what I held on to.

But if Avalon did belong to someone, then why did no one put out missing cat announcements? Why hadn't anyone called nearby veterinarians or pet shelters for help?

I also wondered if it was possible that Avalon had become neurotic because he'd lost his humans with whom he shared a close bond. It was a question that would never get answered.

Meanwhile, Avalon out-endured everyone's patience. They pleaded with me to give him away.

I didn't budge.

No matter how impossible Avalon became, I just understood how he functioned. Abandoning him again was the worst thing I could do to this cat. I refused to treat him that way.

Then, several months later, I found a flyer in the mailbox.

Male cat lost on Avenue Lebon in Oudergem.
White with ginger patches.
Fifty euros compensation.

The picture on the announcement was of Avalon.

He had a family.
Someone loved him.
I had only one option: return Avalon to his owners. They were probably worried stiff not knowing what happened to their cat. Yet all I could think about was why they hadn't looked for him before. If only they'd phoned one animal shelter or veterinarian in the neighborhood, they would have gotten him back. If they'd distributed the missing cat announcement days or even weeks after he got lost, he would have been home within a few hours.

Why hadn't they done that?

If I were to lose Avalon, I'd search for him immediately and not give up until I knew he was safe.

Was Avalon happy in his former family? I had no idea. The only thing I knew was that I felt so protective of Avalon that I *had* to keep him. I promised myself that I would give this needy cat all the love he deserved, and that I would find a way to turn him into the happiest feline the world had ever known.

So I hid the missing cat announcement and never told Stephan about it. It was the biggest secret I had ever kept from him. It was the biggest secret I had kept from anyone.

PET PEEVES

As the years passed, the feeling that I'd made a mistake by not giving Avalon back to his owners became progressively worse as nothing I did assuaged his discontentment. Ignoring the neighbors' cats had diminished his jealousy, but with four more beings in the apartment demanding my devotion, Avalon's reality was still a far cry from his personal utopia, and new pet peeves were routinely added to his usual problem-seeking behavior.

Small changes often caused major disturbances. When we removed a DVD from the cupboard, or put a pen on the living room table that he wasn't used to seeing there, Avalon pitched himself near the problem area and vocalized his complaints as if he was a muezzin calling to prayer. He only stopped if the space returned back to normal.

Intelligent and calculating as he was, Avalon had also developed a technique to prevent Ballon and Tigris from using *his* litter boxes. Each time he heard the scratch scratch scratch in the litter, he settled into attack mode behind the bathroom wall, wiggled his behind, and leapt onto the other cat as soon as it emerged, making it jump. It worked every...single... time. Proud,

Avalon walked away from the crime scene with his nose pointing airwards.

Borat, our guinea pig, was initially the best one off, but ended up the most miserable. What kept him safe at first was Avalon's fear of rodents. Cats may be considered deadly predators, killing a median of 2.4 billion birds and 12.3 billion mammals a year in the United States alone, but whenever Borat had free range inside the apartment, Avalon went in a large circle around him, avoiding him at all cost.

Eventually, Avalon ferreted out a way to make Borat twinge in distress whenever he approached. It started when I taught Avalon not to throw up on the bed and carpets. Those lessons must have been meaningful, because Avalon didn't vomit in those places anymore. Instead he aimed for the guinea pig's head. As soon as he felt a hairball mounting, Avalon ran as fast as he could toward Borat's cage, leaned in, and puked his heart out.

***

One summer evening, Stephan and I came home from dinner at a nearby Italian restaurant to find that our three cats had disappeared.

Regardless of their activities, they always greeted us at the front door. But today, as we switched on the lights, they were nowhere to be seen. They didn't even come when called.

Fanning across the house, we checked our rooms and closets for telltales of our pets, but not one could be detected. There had been many burglaries in our neighborhood. Maybe the apartment had been broken into, and the cats had run off and couldn't find their way back in. We checked all doors, but they were tightly closed.

When we arrived in the kitchen, a soft line of light greeted us through the darkness. It was coming from the fridge. The door was ajar and the contents spread out over the floor. One important element was missing: the barbecue meat for the next day's garden party.

We followed a trail of food and ripped plastic and foil, and finally arrived into our home office. There, our three cats thrived on a feast of pork chops, spicy sausages, and marinated chicken legs. Though they were supposed to feed a cavalry of six hungry people, hardly anything was left.

If we'd left the barbecue meat out in the open, we could've easily blamed ourselves. But when exactly did cats learn to open a refrigerator? Who was responsible for this well-thought-out mess? Tonight, at least, it seemed as if all three of them were guilty.

Days after the incident, Avalon couldn't get his bowels started. He squatted, strained, stopped and crabbed forward, as if in great discomfort.

We immediately took him to Dr. Henri.

"In his eating frenzy, Avalon might have accidentally swallowed some of the plastic wrapping and foil," he said. "I'll X-ray his intestines to make sure that nothing inhibits the intestinal passage."

As soon as Avalon landed onto the examination table, he behaved like a lion being operated on without anesthetic. Maliciously growling, he poked his claws into the vet who felt for lumps, tears, or obstructions. He resisted being manipulated with all his might. The amount of force he was able to command was startling. Even for an experienced veterinarian like Dr. Henri, Avalon was a challenge.

After looking at the X-ray results, Dr. Henri said, "There is indeed a mass of inorganic material obstructing the passageway toward his intestines. A surgical procedure might be necessary. But before we do anything drastic, let's see if we can eliminate the blockage with glycerin."

The following days I mixed a teaspoon of glycerin with Avalon's wet food. As a result, he was locked inside his litter box for hours on end, producing large quantities of heavily fragrant diarrhea. He came to us for comfort, but he smelled so foul that Stephan and I couldn't let him curl up with us, no matter how much we empathized with him.

The good news was that the obstruction disappeared. A surgical procedure was avoided.

The bad news was that Avalon hadn't learned a thing. He gobbled down everything he could lay his paws on, especially hot peppers, chick peas, canned corn, cheese, plastic bags, and Christmas trees. He'd trade in his favorite Almo Nature chicken meals for those forbidden delicacies.

Not everything went down easily, and Avalon vomited with the ease and regularity of a bulimic. He would let out a loud *Gaaaaaack* in the next room, and by the time we rushed in, there would be another non-comestible item, sitting in a puddle of half-digested kibble on Borat's head.

Meanwhile, the door of the fridge continued to open miraculously. We blocked it with boxes, but an unseen force pushed them away effortlessly as soon as they had arrived. Closing off the door to the kitchen seemed like another solution, but whoever plundered our fridge also knew how to use a door handle.

Who was the culprit?

Being a thief, Ballon was our first pick, but considering he made a hobby out of throwing himself onto non-existent furniture, maybe he wasn't smart enough for this type of behavior. Also, Ballon was pretty straightforward about the stealing. Being sneaky wasn't his style. Tigris, on the other hand, was as interested in food as an anorexic. That left us with the smartest of all three: Avalon. Later, we learned that Turkish Van cats are renowned for opening doors and cabinets.

One evening, Stephan and I watched a movie from the comfort of our bed. When I got thirsty, I went to the kitchen to make a cup of tea.

In the dingy light, Avalon stood next to the fridge, placing his claws meticulously at the door gasket, pulling at it with all his might, while narrowing his eyes like a cartoon character in the middle of a tiring physical activity. Clueless to my presence, he checked out what treasures lay within, and stretched forward to gobble down a pack of hot peppers in the back.

I cleared my throat loudly as he chewed away, and he froze mid-bite, staring at me. Looking like he'd been caught off guard in the middle of a major heist, he just stood there, shamefaced.

Avalon then brought his paw to his mouth in the most theatrical way possible, and started grooming it, turning an innocent face to my accusatory one. *Maybe I can pretend I was doing something else*, was so obviously what he was thinking.

It wasn't the first time he tried to fool me. I caught him fighting with Tigris once, his paw up in the air, ready to strike. As soon as I came in, he brought his lifted paw to his mouth, once more pretending he was cleaning himself.

But that evening, he noticed my admiration for his intelligence and agility. He understood I would be inordinately proud, no matter what trick he pulled. From then on, he opened the fridge whenever he felt like it, regardless if I was present or not.

On a singular occasion Avalon expressed kindness that was so short-lived it could have been easily forgotten.

When he was four years old, Borat went on a hunger strike, refusing everything from kibble to chicory and Alpine hay. Knowing that a guinea pig's intestines shut down entirely after forty-eight hours without food, we took Borat to the vet. Days before he went on a fast, Borat moved his jaws in an unusual manner while nibbling his food, so our presumption was dental problems.

"His teeth are in great shape," the vet assured us. "I'm going to give him a vitamin C injection, but there's nothing more I can do. Guinea pigs are a difficult species, you can never tell whether a treatment is going to work or not."

Borat went from looking normal to skeletal in just two days and we asked a second veterinarian for advice. The result was basically the same. No cause was found, but several life-saving tips were given, such as force-feeding him liquid recovery food and sugar water. Besides that, nothing else could be done.

A third veterinarian made his appearance in the hopes of finding the origin of Borat's rapid decline.

"Of course he's not eating," he said. "How could he? His tongue is stuck because his back teeth have grown over each other."

The problem was quickly resolved, yet Borat's loss of appetite persisted.

We spent the remainder of the day in bed with Borat resting on my chest. During all that time, Avalon gave the space for both of us. No matter how possessive he'd been, no matter how often he'd pushed the other pets off me in an attempt to usurp their place, that day he didn't intrude on our time together. Avalon accepted his second-fiddle status with good-natured resignation.

During the night, Borat's condition worsened. Having draped himself across my neck, he peeped in agony and gasped for air.

Avalon sidled up next to him and gave his little friend soft licks on the head. It was the first and only time Avalon showed kindness toward another creature.

He reminded me of Oscar, the cat who lived at a nursing home. He could sense when one of the residents was near death and would sit on their bed during their last moments. Maybe Avalon could sense it too, because Borat slipped away several hours later.

In the weeks that followed, Avalon allowed me space to grieve and didn't force affection on me. I couldn't wait to unveil more of that empathy. But the question remained: How was I ever going coax that empathy from him?

A NEW START

Ten years after meeting Stephan, I ended our relationship. I wasn't tired of him, but I was tired of being down on luck. Because most of my struggles had started around the same time as our relationship, I had come to associate the two.

All I wanted was to break out of the negative spiral that didn't allow me to move forward. I needed a fresh start, centered on opportunities and happiness. And the only remaining way to force a change was to let go of the man I loved.

For a long time, Stephan knew I was slipping away. Because he was still in love with me, he bribed me into staying by surprising me with city trips, the destination kept a secret until we arrived at the airport. He treated me to favorite restaurants, and bought me presents. But the only thing that could make me happy was the only thing he couldn't offer me, and that was some time off from the relationship.

I read somewhere that, "Sometimes you have to let a person go so they can grow. Because, over the course of their lives, it is not what you do for them, but what you have taught them to do for themselves that will make them a successful human being."

I needed to comprehend I was fully responsible for everything that had/hadn't happened, and there wasn't anyone or anything to blame except myself.

But no matter how much I longed for a new life, I felt unable to free myself from the relationship. Perhaps deep down, I didn't want to walk away. There were still moments of tenderness, for it was clear how deeply and loyally we loved each other.

The Brussels International Fantastic Film Festival, the event through which I had met both Stephan and Avalon, had become a good indicator of my progress. That year, it would have been exactly ten years since my life had stalled. Ten years was a long time for accomplishing nothing. The festival reminded me of my ideals. In the beginning, I used to feel excitement and motivation to work on my projects. Now it only fed my discontentment.

I wanted my next year to be a year of making things happen, a year of making every day count, a year of becoming exactly who I wanted to be. Because I didn't want to be in the same spot next year, thinking the same thoughts, and getting nothing done.

So one afternoon, right before the festival started, I rented a new apartment and called Stephan to tell him I wasn't coming home. It was a spontaneous decision, yet, as contradictory as it may sound, also one that sprang from years of deliberate thought.

***

"It's you and me now, Avalon," I said as we settled into our new two-bedroom apartment overlooking the park of Zaventem. Close enough to the Belgian capital to give its inhabitants the feeling to be part of something bigger, yet surrounded by so much green and tranquility that people hardly ever left town except for work, Zaventem was also the place where I grew up.

Returning to my native village unconsciously underlined my desire to go back to who I was when I left ten years ago and to continue my life's journey from there. During the first months, I continued to feel discouraged. Everything I undertook was followed by new streaks of bad luck. I told myself that the idea of a life change had been ridiculous. Obviously it was impossible to start over and actually be happy, even in the narrow terms by which I had come to define happiness. This time, though, I no longer had someone or something else to blame. If there were a way out, it would be up to me to find it.

However, the positive impact of the break-up on Avalon made it all worthwhile. It was the best thing that could have happened to him. Not only did he adapt quickly, he also transformed in a way I could never have imagined. I knew he wanted to be an exclusive cat, but I had no idea how much he would bloom if the world around us were to evaporate into thin air. Now that it was just the two of us, I didn't recognize him anymore. In a good way.

First there was his newfound joy in playing. Avalon had a basket full of toys he had never touched--bouncing balls, catnip mice, squeaky toys--but now he suddenly seemed to have discovered the word "fun." His favorite toy was a purple plastic wheel containing a ball. He could reach through slits along the top and sides of the wheel, and push around the ball inside. Avalon quickly became obsessed, convinced he could figure out a way to liberate it. When he couldn't catch the ball, the game would end with his frustrating, deep-from-the-chest growl.

Another game he enjoyed was chasing a fishing rod. I had to move it slowly at first so he could watch the fish at the end of the rod and prepare an attack. Then I would yank it forward, and he chased after it like a mad cat. Avalon also loved how I moved the rod over the furniture until it disappeared behind a corner.

The new apartment came with a nearby pond, and with that pond came flies. They immeasurably added to Avalon's enjoyment. It didn't take long before he became a master in fly destruction. First he would trail the fly with his gaze for a few seconds. His hugely dilated eyes moved back and forth in perfect time with the flies' irregular movements, his ears pricked up as high as they could go. Nothing could distract him. In his tense pose, he looked like he calculated an intricate plan of when and how to strike. When he finally did pounce, he would whap out a front paw, and scoop the hapless fly up in his mouth. Fly destruction was an art form that Avalon practiced to perfection.

But most of all, Avalon and I became closer than ever. He followed me around like a lap dog, making sure he was always in the same room with me. He jammed his head through the shower curtain for a drink as I bathed, tested my food when I cooked dinner, typed the occasional gibberish when I wrote, snuggled when we watched a movie together, and used his paw as a bookmark when I read. His favorite part of the day was when I went to the bedroom--whether it was to sleep, read, or write--because that meant I would be with him for a long time. As soon as I stepped into bed, I would hear the *clip-clip* of Avalon's footsteps on the floorboards trailing behind me. For the majority of our first winter, we huddled in bed, keeping the chill at bay by wrapping ourselves in thick blankets and one another.

He always slept for exactly as long as I slept. That moment when you open your eyes in the morning, but you immediately doze back off, that's when Avalon woke me up with a session of purring and head butts. If I turned to sleep some more, he tapped me on the face until I gave him my undivided attention. We always cuddled like that for at least ten minutes before I climbed out of bed.

Food was never his number one priority. I always gave him his cherished Almo Nature dinners first thing in the morning, but before heading off to his bowl, he waited for me on the sofa to love on me some more. Only when I started to work on my laptop did he hobble off to eat. After his meal, he snuggled up next to me when I worked on my book, making sure our bodies touched at all times. If I dared to move, he dabbed a paw in my direction, nudging me to come back to him. We were sandwiched so close together it was hard to believe we were two separate beings.

The rhythms of our lives had adjusted themselves to one another. We were completely in sync. We even sneezed at the same time, though scientists agree that colds are not interchangeable between cats and humans. There was no denying this new, deeper symmetry between us.

The dark gloom that continually covered his eyes in the past had given way to a tender gaze. Whenever I kissed him, he had this contented but tuckered-out look on his face, as though life got no better than this. His muscles and posture, once tense, had relaxed. Now that he was loved exclusively, Avalon finally was where he wanted to be in life. He had blossomed into the cat he was meant to be.

And I had started to blossom into the girl I was meant to be. Many people, when they feel unloved, turn to God because the Bible tells them that God loves them as if they were the only ones who had ever mattered. I turned to my cat. I had been longing for love and appreciation ever since I was born, but believed that I would remain unlikeable if I didn't attain that imagined state of flawlessness. Now, for the first time, I had found that unconditional love. Looking into my cat's eyes that clearly read, *I adore you*, I finally felt appreciated.

STRANGERS

I had started my new life in March, and in December I published my first novel, *Drowned Sorrow*. Though it was a suspenseful chiller--the story of a remote town where water had become a supernatural element that could think, move, and kill--it contained many elements that had been prominent in my life with Stephan, mainly the feelings of being locked in by the ones you love, and holding onto them while equally wanting to escape.

Soon after its release, *Drowned Sorrow* caught the interest of several filmmakers. It didn't take long before the project was "in development," and rumor had it Drew Barrymore was slated to direct.

Thanks to my professional success and the comfort I found in Avalon's devotion to me, I finally dared to go out and socialize again. I was no longer ashamed of myself.

On April 18, I was invited to the Brussels International Fantastic Film Festival for my first panel discussion and book signing. Exactly one year earlier, I had wanted my life to be transformed before this event, and it had in ways I never believed possible.

A thrill of electricity sent the blood tingling around my veins and I permitted myself a smile. I was finally living and not merely surviving. I couldn't help but feel an overwhelming gratefulness for my blessings that had occurred over the course of one year. After the book signing, I met Lucky McKee of whom I'd been a fan for years. I was particularly fond of his movie *May*, probably because I recognized myself in the female lead and her struggles to connect with the people around her.

"You look like my ex-girlfriend. She died," Lucky said as a way of introducing himself. Despite the awkwardness of the situation, we talked the entire night about loneliness, insecurities, and animals.

After the festival, he emailed me to say how much he had loved *Drowned Sorrow*, which he had read on the plane back home. "I'm currently preparing a short story anthology in collaboration with Rue Morgue Magazine. It would be great if you could contribute a story as well," he continued. "Several household names are already attached to the project."

With Avalon glued next to me at all times, I began to work on *The Strangers Outside*, a survival tale that included a home invasion, killers in monk clothes, and a supernatural twist.

However, the anthology never saw the light of day. It seemed as if *The Strangers Outside* missed its opportunity.

***

Several months later, I attended the movie premiere of the French language film *Combat avec l'ange*. Nothing glamorous. The venue was a small cinema that specialized in independent releases.

"I heard they're calling you the female version of Stephen King," editor Philippe Geus told me over some champagne and toast. "I love Stephen King. I definitely have to read *Drowned Sorrow* someday."

He did, and several weeks later he called to say he wanted to discuss a possible project.

Philippe and I met a few days later on the covered terrace of a bar in Brussels. The sky had turned an odd shade of olive gray and an ominous black thunderhead formed several miles to the east. While the rain pelted the shed above us, we discussed our inspirations and aspirations.

"Do you have something similar to *Drowned Sorrow?* Something that could be adapted into a short film?" Philippe Geus asked. "I'd like to direct my first film, but I can't find a good supernatural story."

I immediately thought of *The Strangers Outside.* "I wrote a short story for an anthology. The book won't be released, so it's still available."

"What's it about?"

"It's a story of survival. Two sisters trapped in a remote cottage by ominous figures in monk clothes. They search for a way to escape while their assailants move closer."

"Can you send me this? It might be just what I'm looking for."

Philippe Geus emailed me a couple of days later to announce his decision: *The Strangers Outside* would become his first film.

As soon as I agreed, the development of *The Strangers Outside* was on its rails. The first weeks were dedicated to script meetings and rewrites. As Philippe Geus wanted to work with Belgian actor Pierre Lekeux, we replaced the two sisters from the original story with a crippled man and his daughter. That meant every single line of dialogue had to be rewritten, as well as the ending since the original one was more philosophical than visual.

After that, the production moved forward at the speed of light.

I asked Philippe Geus if Avalon could get a cameo in the movie, just a split second of him ambling near the house.

"I have a better idea," Philippe said. "Why don't we give Avalon a real part in the film?"

His eyes lit up with little stars, like a child's when gifted with his favorite toy. "Avalon will be the first victim. I want to see him butchered by those evil monks."

HOLLYWOOD'S NEXT BIG THING

Filming of *The Strangers Outside* took place in August and September 2010. Avalon joined the set for two days. The location: a vacation cabin in the woods of Sint-Katelijne-Waver, a place where shadows came alive and danced with the rare patches of light. The perfect site for a horror movie.

Outside the vacation cabin, the film crew prepared for action. Camera tripods and lights were set up. An actor in monk clothes smoked his last cigarette before the shoot.

Two large tables with food and drinks sat in the shade, each bottle of water labeled with the name of an actor or crew member. Avalon had a bottle all for himself.

Avalon was remarkably at ease on set. He examined the vacation cabin for about half an hour, sniffing his way through the dusty corners, before settling into a deep sleep on the couch.

While everyone fawned over Avalon and fed him snacks from the buffet table, the director gave us a quick rundown of the scene to come. "The camera focuses on Avalon lying on the coffee table. In the background, through the windows, we see actors Pierre Lekeux and Iulia Nastase arriving home. Avalon follows their movements with his head as they move from one side of the house to the other. When the front door opens, Avalon jumps off the table to greet them."

"Avalon won't do that," I said. "Just like children, cats are uncontrollable. It's a great idea for a scene, but I'm afraid you'll have to come up with something less demanding."

Apparently, I didn't know my cat very well, because Avalon did *exactly* what was expected of him.

The scene was shot several times in a row and Avalon never missed a beat.

In another scene, while eating his Schesir dinner, Avalon suddenly had to look up in panic. The fear in his eyes looked genuine. He was perfect.

Sitting at the dining table, actor Pierre Lekeux watched Avalon with incomprehensibility and admiration, shaking his head in denial. "I need at least twenty minutes to prepare a scene, to enter a certain state of mind. But this cat nails it in a matter of seconds. Avalon's the best actor on set. He's even better than *me*."

Pierre was right. Avalon had this air--he carried himself in a certain way, very much aware of his charisma. He was a natural performer. A miniature star.

***

The following day, we were in the middle of the woods surrounded by blackboard sky. No lights whatsoever. Yet, Philippe Geus insisted on filming Avalon leaving the cottage through the front door. If Avalon charged outside, we might never be able to recover him, so I tried to talk Philippe out of it.

"Think about it," he said. "Avalon will be attacked on the porch. If the audience doesn't see him leaving the cottage, it'll be considered a continuity error. We don't really have a choice but to film this scene."

It all made perfect sense, of course, but it didn't eliminate my motherly concerns.

I convinced around ten people to stand nearby with large blankets to prevent Avalon from leaving the porch and haul him back if necessary.

During the first takes, my heart nearly stopped, but Avalon understood more than I thought. As soon as Philippe Geus called, "Cut!" Avalon simply returned inside, looking at me with an air of, *What are you so scared of? I know what I'm doing.*

It didn't matter how many takes had to be done; Avalon's reaction was always the same.

The entire crew thought this was highly amusing and took advantage of the opportunity to film Avalon from as many angles as possible: lying down, standing, jumping, moving around. Avalon was ready to perform.

And I just watched in astonished silence.

***

But even the best actors need a stand-in once in a while. Being gutted and smashed against a window was not something we wanted to subject Avalon to.

In collaboration with special effects man Pascal Berger, Philippe Geus concocted a puppet in Avalon's likeness and filled it with fresh blood and guts. It would then be thrown against the window, burst open, and splatter the surroundings.

For the audience, the scene lasted only a second. For the crew, it took an entire night to film.

The reason it took so long was because the action happened too quickly to understand what was going on. The special effects team experimented with the force they used to thrust the fake Avalon against the window, but the stand-in never stayed glued to the pane long enough to distinguish anything on camera. In between each take, they cleaned the puppet and re-filled it with blood and entrails, delaying the shoot.

By morning, the crew finally got it right. Unfortunately, another scene had to be filmed in which Pierre Lekeux escapes the hooded figures, passing a now unrecognizable blood-soaked Avalon on the porch.

"We should have used the real Avalon for these gore scenes," Philippe Geus muttered. "He would have done it right from the first take and we wouldn't be behind schedule."

**

The Strangers Outside (now just called *Strangers*) premiered on April 12, 2013 at the Imagine Film Festival in Amsterdam, the Netherlands.

"Look at page seventy-six," Philippe Geus said when handing me the festival catalogue.

Expecting to see the summary of *Strangers*, I scrolled through the pages to number seventy-six. Big was my surprise to see that Avalon's picture adorned the page. The Imagine Film Festival had chosen a screenshot with Avalon to represent the film in their catalogue.

Strangers also led to another step in Avalon's path to stardom. Music producer Alex Corbi used footage from the film for one of his music videos, and, to my delight, even named the song after him.

Needless to say I was proud of my little celebrity.

LOVE ETERNAL

Many people are obsessed with leaving their mark on the world, whether it's through art or children. I never cared about being remembered; I never cared if my stories got lost over time, or that I'd never have children to continue my genes. But since Avalon's cinematic stardom, I reveled how all the spotlights were on him. Thanks to *Strangers*, a little spark of Avalon would remain. The movie had made him and our love eternal.

But his "celebrity status" also reflected how I regarded Avalon--on a pedestal with lights shining on him. It was my way of expressing that awe. And when the buzz around *The Strangers Outside* faded, I looked for new ways to voice my admiration.

In interviews, Avalon permeated all conversation:

"What is the one thing you never go without?"
"My cat."
"What three famous people would you like to spend time with on a deserted island?"
"I'd rather be with my cat."
"What would you brag about if you had a license to brag?"

"I would brag about my cat."

"Is there something I should've asked you about that I haven't?"

"You should've asked me about my cat."

Avalon even sneaked his way into the press on his own behalf. If I was being interviewed at home, journalists were welcomed to Avalon's hysterical antics: bouncing off walls and furniture like a magic ball, whining for attention, racing in blurred circles around the apartment, breaking the journalist's belongings, and doing memorable impersonations of a Tasmanian Devil. Those feline shenanigans were funnier to write about than more serious literary conversations.

During a Radio 2 interview, the reporter asked me if Avalon would make more appearances in my work after *Strangers*. I replied, "Alfred Hitchcock can be seen in every one of his movies. In my case, it's not me but Avalon who can be spotted." As I spoke the words, I realized I was never going to write another story that didn't contain at least a little bit of Avalon.

Soon afterwards, I wrote two short film scripts – *Next to Her* and *GPS with Benefits*, both of which contained parts for Avalon. In *Next to Her*, an eighty-four-year-old man visits his terminally ill wife in the hospital. A daily lunch is the only thing they still share. But the woman's attention fades toward the ghost of her cat, Avalon, whom she sees walking around in her hospital room.

Including Avalon in *GPS with Benefits* was trickier. It was about a man who tries out a modern GPS device that punishes him whenever he makes a mistake. Every scene in this short film takes place in the car. I did, however, ask the director to use a picture of Avalon for a cat food ad that distracts the driver.

In all of these films, Avalon was only a secondary character. I dreamed about giving him his own story. The idea didn't mingle with my supernatural thrillers, but I reasoned that if Dean Koontz and William Burroughs could write stories about their pets, so could I.

I'd started to develop a feature film called *Santa Claws*, a sort of *Home Alone* with cats. The film would include Avalon in every frame, but if I was honest with myself, I knew such a project would be hard to finance and set up in Belgium. Even if it did work out, chances were slim that Avalon would be allowed to take the lead. There were just too many decision makers involved.

As my mind raced to find ways to eternalize Avalon, the possibilities soon stretched beyond the boundaries of the movie business. Some of the scenes of *Santa Claws* translated into small cartoonish story ideas. The inspiration was there, but I lacked talent to illustrate those stories.

As soon as I announced that I was looking for an illustrator, I was introduced to Allan Beurms. His sample illustrations were adorable and matched my own ideas.

Two months later, on December 13, Allan and I tested the waters by publishing the first Avalon cartoons on a blog. The site premiered with *Shark Attack*, a funny cartoon in which Avalon daydreams about being in a restaurant that serves shark. Decked out in diving gear, he plunges into an aquarium, only to be hunted by the shark instead.

In only a few months, over ten thousand readers kept up with Avalon's cat cartoons. Readers sent in love letters, ranging from a simple, *I love you, Avalon*, to more elaborate writings on one's obsession with my cat. From now on, Christmas cards were no longer addressed to me, but to my cat. It was exactly how I wanted it to be.

***

A couple of weeks into the New Year, I got a phone call from the organization of Dijlelanddag, a yearly local event featuring concerts, circus performances, guided walks, literary readings, and stalls with local dishes. They'd seen a feature about my work in a Belgian magazine and they asked me to write a creepy children's tale that I could read aloud during the event.

"We'd like you to bring Avalon when you read the story to the children," the organizer said. "He's a popular little guy; the kids will love him."

My first reaction was that of a concerned mother. "Maybe ... but I want Avalon's safety and wellbeing to be the main priority. He needs fresh water and food, and a place where he can't escape into the crowd."

"We'll make a concerted point of ensuring we'll pamper him like royalty."

They kept to their word.

Dijlelanddag took place on May 29 in the park Jan van Ruusbroec in Hoeilaert. It was a particularly hot day for this time of year, and the car ride was torture for Avalon. He was on my lap in the passenger seat, panting and soaking in every whiff of air coming through the slightly open window. What had come over me to even consider bringing him to such an event?

On arrival, I immediately asked the organization for a bowl of water. Luckily, the place of our literary reading--a 15th century chapel belonging to a castle--was cool enough to make Avalon feel better in no time.

The chapel also matched the safety requirements. It was small, yet big enough to host a class of children; Avalon could move freely without the risk of getting lost. If someone wanted to enter, they had to first make sure that Avalon was back in his carrier.

As soon as Avalon had recovered from the tiring car ride, he explored the chapel at his own pace while I rehearsed the story I was about to tell. I had chosen a tale about a child who gets nightly visits from a malevolent ghost. The child's cat, Avalon, acts as a protector and keeps the specter at a distance. When the parents are fed up with their daughter's supposed nightmares, they punish her by keeping Avalon in another room for the night. The girl won't survive.

Just before the arrival of the first batch of children at 2:30, I put Avalon back into his carrier. Once the children were inside, the door closed, and Avalon roamed freely.

Pets usually don't like to "work," but just like with the filming of *Strangers,* I only had to look at Avalon's body language to know that the public appearance had his seal of approval.

As soon as he saw his audience, Avalon struck a pose. With his nose pointing upwards and his paws stretched forward, he looked akin to a self-conscious girl trying to appear sexy for a photo shoot.

The children greeted him like a celebrity. They cooed over him, caressing his soft fur.

And Avalon?

He relished their attention. Once more, it became clear how much this cat needed to be loved.

After his first tough years of being ignored and even downright hated, Avalon had his revenge--he was a star, and everyone admired him.

COMMUNICATION

People who never had pets often say it's impossible for humans and cats to communicate with each other, and trying to understand them is merely a form of anthropomorphism. While I couldn't have a conversation with Avalon about the latest scientific discoveries, we had both learned to understand each other regarding far more important things in life. The many signals he emitted told me exactly what mood he was in, when he was hungry, and what he needed at any particular moment.

Far more verbal than any other cat I had known, Avalon expressed every frustration, every emotion, every wish in a set of decibel-heavy meows. Ever since the early days, a continuous soundtrack had been added to my life. Even in his sleep, he wasn't able to shut up. His nightmares made him mumble and hiss, his paws twitching, his shoulders flinching, probably fighting with other felines over my attention.

Before adopting Avalon, I complained that Ballon and Tigris weren't vocal enough. Now I wanted nothing more than a few minutes of silence. Where only little peeps emerged when Ballon and Tigris opened their mouths, Avalon honed his ability to converse with an incessant range of complex sounds. A repetitive atonal mrow, mrow, mrow meant *Get out. Get out. Get out.* It would only be discontinued if my visitors left the apartment. Usually, that sufficed to drive everyone to distraction.

He let out a long beseeching yowl that meant, *I need cuddles,* and a similar, slightly more prolonged yowl that meant, *I need cuddles in bed.* A tiny, plaintive warble that went up at the end, like a sentence punctuated by a question mark, was uttered whenever I prepared to leave by putting on my coat, but when I came back I was greeted with a set of happy, half-swallowed little mews. A piercing, persistent me-oooow indicated that Avalon was about to vomit. Irritable as he was, Avalon had also developed a sound for frustration: a deep, long-stretched growl that he muttered whenever he stumbled over his paws, or couldn't catch the toy or fly. His loudest, most guttural snarl detonated after each visit to the litter box. Poo, in particular, made him dart around the apartment, bellowing like a raging Tasmanian Devil. A fascinating sight for visitors.

My favorite was a series of loud and drawn-out coos resembling those of a pigeon, which he produced whenever he was deliriously happy. He cooed each time I brought home a pot of fresh catnip, when visitors left the house, or when I went to bed (which meant the two of us would be alone together for many uninterrupted hours).

Avalon was also capable of speaking a few words of French. They were well-pronounced meows that coincidentally resembled the French vocabulary, but it had people fooled every time.

Whenever Avalon was hungry, he had a way of calling me that sounded like a French child's relentless chanting of *Maman. Maman. Maman.* "Is your cat calling you Mom?" friends or family members would often ask.

Returning from the kitchen with a full bowl of food, I'd ask him, "Qui veut manger?" (Who wants to eat?) Avalon would trot off after me saying, "Moi. Moi. Moi." (Me. Me. Me.)

And he was a real fashionista too. Whenever I asked him, "How do you like my new dress?" I got the response, "Wow."

Those seemingly human sounds reminded me of a scene in Dean Koontz' book *A Big Little Life* in which the author's dog Trixie repeatedly produced the sound "Baw" (sounding like "Ball") every time he passed the tennis court and wasn't allowed to play with the balls.

But in reality, Avalon didn't need language to make his demands clear. We were like an old couple living together for so long they finish each other's sentences and know what the other is thinking without uttering a word.

A few months after the shooting of *The Strangers Outside*, I had the feeling that something was wrong with him. I wasn't sure where it came from. Avalon's eyes were lively, his fur shiny, his body firm, and his behavior energetic. He was also eating and drinking well. Nothing out of the ordinary. Still the thought of him being ill persisted.

It may have been just the negativity born of a sleepless night, a fraction of my imagination, an unconscious fear of losing my special cat. Or maybe our close bond made me pick up on changes so small my conscious mind couldn't grasp them.

Whatever the cause, I took Avalon to the veterinary clinic to be sure.

HYPERTHYROIDISM

Like most cats, Avalon had never been a good patient. When the technician at the veterinary clinic wanted to collect a blood sample, things got out of hand. Avalon expressed his displeasure by growling and screaming and hissing and clawing violently around him. Not able to handle such an uncontrollable beast by himself, the technician left the room to ask for help.

His colleague thought that wearing thick rubber gloves would do the trick, but after Avalon's claws missed his cheek by only a few inches, his confident attitude turned into anxious glances.

Fifteen minutes later, six veterinarians, all wearing thick protection gloves and covered with blankets, attempted to hold Avalon still so they could inject him with a tranquilizer. It was of no use.

"This cat needs holy water instead of tranquilizer," one of them said.

An image of *The Exorcist* sprang to mind – a possessed Reagan being tied to the bed, tossing savagely, the priests sprinkling her with holy water. What happened here at the veterinary clinic was hardly any different.

Eventually, one of them administered the injection, and Avalon fell asleep. A loud, collective sigh of relief issued across the room.

"Has Avalon ever been tested for hyperthyroidism?" the chief veterinarian asked.

"Not that I know of. I have a file with the history of all of Avalon's previous blood works with me."

I handed him the file, which he studied for a few minutes.

"Indeed. He has never been tested," he said.

"What are the symptoms?"

"Weight loss, restlessness, excessive water drinking and urination, vomiting, diarrhea, difficulty breathing."

"He doesn't have any of those. He vomits and urinates a lot, but he has always done that."

"In the beginning it's possible that you don't see any of the symptoms, but given his old age, he's very much at risk. In fact, it's one of the more common illnesses in older cats, and it may affect his heart and kidneys as well."

"Avalon's not that old," I defended.

"The average cat with hyperthyroidism is thirteen years of age."

"He's only eleven."

"That's not an eleven-year-old cat. He's at least two years older."

"How can you tell?"

"The eyes are less sharp. His limbs are rigid."

"Avalon's first vet said he was about one and a half years old when I found him. That makes him about eleven now."

"Age is difficult to determine. We can only estimate, and I'd say this cat is *at least* thirteen years old."

If it were true that cats aged seven years for every one of ours, Avalon would now be 91 years old. Another more positive theory stated that the first two years of a cat's life equaled twenty-four human years; after that, each cat year would be roughly the same as four human years. That put Avalon on the downward slope to seventy.

In any case, I might lose him sooner than I'd expected, maybe even months from now. The only thing I could do was to delay the moment by giving him the best possible care.

"The T-4 test requires a separate blood sample, so we'd better take that now while he's asleep," the veterinarian insisted.

I agreed, and a new blood sample was taken.

The technician gave him another injection to let him come out of his sedation. A few minutes later, Avalon woke, and we returned home.

Back in our apartment, I coaxed Avalon out of his cat box. Still groggy, he did a few drunken steps forward, then stumbled over his paws, and fell. I scooped him up and placed him on the bed where I cradled him for several hours until he was back to his normal self. The early spring sunshine sought its way inside and warmed our entangled bodies.

For the next few days, there was nothing I could do except wait for the lab results.

***

The veterinarian called me a week later to confirm that Avalon was indeed suffering from hyperthyroidism.

I had believed that Avalon would remain healthy if I gave him the best possible food and care. I had given him organic food, avoided unnecessary medicines, provided fresh water daily, and gave him all the love he needed. Still, it didn't prevent him from getting old and sick. Wasn't I doing enough? Was I somehow responsible for his illness?

I had no intention of letting Avalon's hyperthyroidism shorten the amount of time we had together.

In the course of my life I had met several cats well into their twenties. I had once known a twenty-two-year-old cat that suffered from the feline immunodeficiency virus FIV. Scrawny he was, but he didn't suffer any discomfort. If such a cat lived that long, then, maybe, I could take Avalon over the median finish line as well. He already was above average in all other aspects of his life, so why not?

The press, too, was full of stories about cats that defied the statistics. One cat I read about, Crème Puff, was born on August 3, 1967, and lived until August 6, 2005. An amazing 38 years and 3 days. He wasn't the only one. Pinky, born in 1989, survived cancer and an amputated leg, and had no intention of leaving his owners just yet.

Any disease could become manageable with knowledge and a well-thought-out plan, I reasoned. So in the weeks following the diagnosis, I read everything I could find on hyperthyroidism. I wanted every piece of medical information, every fact, every opinion, every diagnosis, every test result. I was on a mission to save Avalon. The center of my world changed.

The first question on my mind: Why did Avalon get hyperthyroidism?

The main factor, it appeared, came from chemicals. Fire retardant chemicals in particular seemed to be the culprit. Its worldwide use in carpets, upholstery, and mattresses roughly paralleled the spread of feline hyperthyroidism. This could explain why the disease was more common in indoor cats. Also electronic equipment, vaccines, light toxicity, fish, seafood, corn, and wheat were often mentioned as a cause.

I learned as much as I could on both traditional and alternative cures. I read about hormone pills, radioactive iodine treatments, surgical removal of the thyroid gland, pulsed electro-magnetic therapy, acupuncture, EFT, raw food diets, and supplements such as turmeric, Coenzyme Q10, apple cider vinegar, royal jelly, and aloe vera juice.

As traditional treatments were considered dangerous and alternative remedies inefficient, I discussed the various options with four different veterinarians. All of them contradicted each other.

The veterinarian who diagnosed Avalon with hyperthyroidism, recommended treating him with hormone pills. But weren't chemicals the major cause of his problems? Was it wise to put even more of those in his body by means of pills? He also warned me not to put him on a raw food diet as this contained more iodine than canned food or kibble and would lead to more stimulation of the thyroid.

On the other hand, Avalon's first veterinarian, Dr. Henri, suggested surgical removal of the swollen thyroid gland. Yet, a third one advised against surgery, saying Avalon's heart had weakened and he would surely succumb to the procedure.

"Absolutely no pills or surgery. That will kill him," said the fourth and last veterinarian. "Changing Avalon's diet to raw food and getting him on vitamins and herbal supplements will boost his immune system and should be enough to turn his hyperthyroidism around."

Because of all the conflicting views, I didn't know what to do or who to believe. I had started with the desire to take control, but the more I learned, the more I realized the disease was out of my control. I wanted to protect Avalon, but all I saw was potential danger. My ultimate decision had to come down to intuition, to doing what felt right.

After careful consideration, I decided on getting the best of both worlds: I gave Avalon two half hormone pills a day, one in the morning and one in the evening, served with raw food and an array of varying supplements including brewer's yeast, honey, grapefruit seed extract, turmeric, Coenzyme Q10, Omega 3, elderberry syrup, apple cider vinegar, barley grass, and probiotics.

I equally thought about alternative treatments such as acupuncture and reiki, but none of the practitioners worked outside their clinics and I didn't want to stress Avalon by getting him out of the apartment every week.

***

One month after the diagnosis, I booked Avalon in for a new check-up. I hated having to put him through another round of sedation, so I asked the vet if an alternative existed. The technician gave me an oral tranquilizer to give Avalon twenty minutes before the appointment. The pill was said to be less harmful than full sedation.

Ten minutes after I gave him the pill, the effects settled in. His eyes wide and terrified, he looked at me from the middle of the hallway, babbling in an attempt to call my attention. He unsteadily wiggled over in my direction, but after a few cautious steps, sank to his paws. He didn't protest when I picked him up to put him inside his carrier.

The veterinarian looked relieved when I told him that Avalon was already sedated. I smiled at the idea he was considered an irreverent beast, while with me he was the gentlest being I'd ever come across.

I stopped smiling when I realized that even the tranquilizer couldn't keep Avalon under control. History repeated itself with several technicians being called in for help until full sedation was once more needed to be able to take a blood sample.

I couldn't keep doing this to Avalon. I feared that more trips to the hospital would turn fatal.

Luckily for him, the new blood-works showed that his treatment was working and that his hyperthyroidism was under control. He didn't need to go back to the hospital for at least another six months to a year.

Yet I had come to understand that Avalon's life had an expiry date, that our love would only be temporary. What was once a distant future had now become so close it was almost palpable. It was only yesterday, or so it seemed, that he had come to me as a young cat. Now he was getting old, and these could very well be our last years together.

My feelings for Avalon were goaded into full expression at this realization, as if my devotion to him had only been dormant up until then. As needy for affection as he was, Avalon soaked up my love as a sponge and gave it back to me tenfold. In return, his devotion amplified my attachment, which led once more to an increase of his adulation. It was a vicious circle, but one in which we were glad to be stuck. It didn't take long before we clung to each other like duct tape, never leaving each other's side. Our souls had merged.

Caring for this cat, I had the feeling that this was the one thing I was meant to do in this life. The one thing I was so obviously created to do, that it simply felt like breathing.

"Promise you'll stay with me for many more years," I said.

I wished and hoped that I could trade in my own happiness for a few more years with my cat.

It may not have been a realistic thing to hope for, but it was exactly what happened.

GRANDFATHER

I knew Avalon and I were a team that couldn't be torn apart, that what we shared was a once-in-a-lifetime bond. What I didn't know was that our relationship had the possibility to grow even stronger and that he was about to become the cornerstone of my life when things would get tough.

When my grandfather got diagnosed with intestinal cancer with metastases in the liver, the outcome, certainly at my grandfather's age, was predictable. I made it my business to improve his wellbeing as much as possible and to accompany him to the hospital for chemotherapy treatments.

I owed him that emotional backing. Through vacations, restaurants, and good wine, he had taught me to enjoy the little things in life. He had also introduced me to the art of storytelling by inventing his own *Laurel and Hardy* bedtime stories when I was a child.

For months it seemed as if he was still strong enough to fight the disease, but by the end of the year, the sparkle in my grandfather's eyes died down at the same pace the Christmas lights started to illuminate the streets. Where only months before, he looked like a young Vincent Price, now he was a withering old man at the mercy of nature.

However, cancer wasn't the real cause of his deterioration. It was the chemotherapy that killed not only the cancer cells, but my grandfather as well. It was like a contest, a survival of the fittest. In my grandfather's case, the chemo was on the winning side of the game. I feared that he wouldn't even make the end of the year if he was submitted to any more chemicals.

I asked his oncologist to reconsider the treatment and within the hour, they got him a room where they would sort out his medication and examine the possibilities.

As soon as he entered the hospital room, hallucinations replaced my grandfather's sanity. Apparently this occurs often when older patients are confronted with a change of scenery. He saw the spirits of his deceased dog and sister, and repeated the title of his favorite TV program for at least twenty minutes. Mostly, however, he cried because he believed he was held hostage and wanted to go home.

Each day at the hospital was worse than the one before.

Five days later, I made another decision. "He's coming home with us."

"The doctor said they're not finished with the exams," my grandmother argued. "He has to stay at least until the end of the week."

"If he stays here, he'll be dead by the end of the week."

She shook her head in denial. "I only listen to what the doctor says."

"Can't you see he's getting worse? If he's not coming home today, he never will."

"But what if he dies? I don't want to be alone with him when that happens."

I thought about my grandfather's plea to go home. "We have to respect his last wish," I said. "I'll be there for you every day. I'll arrange a hospital bed and nurses and everything, but *please*, don't leave him here."

"Do you promise?"

"I promise."

A little later, we met with my grandfather's oncologist to look at the options.

"The chemotherapy has halted the spread, but it won't be enough to put the disease into remission," the oncologist said with sickbed politeness. "The best option is to remove the tumor as well as the surrounding tissue in both the intestines and liver."

"That's more than half of both organs, am I correct?"

The oncologist nodded.

"What's the survival rate of such an operation?"

"About fifteen percent."

"And in my grandfather's current state of health?"

The oncologist pondered the question, and avoided answering altogether. "It's the only way to remove the cancer."

"But the operation will almost certainly kill him?"

Silence again. Then, "Yes."

"If he doesn't undergo the operation, how much time will he have left?" my grandmother asked.

"It may be a few months. Probably, a few weeks. No one can tell." He continued, "Why don't you discuss the options together, see if you want to risk the operation or if you just want to enjoy the time you have left together?"

We exited the hospital ten minutes later, my grandmother and I sustaining my grandfather on each side.

"So what are we going to do now?" my grandmother asked.

I looked at my grandfather for an answer. "You're the only one who can decide whether you want the operation or not, Grandpa."

"All I want is to be with the two of you for as long as possible," he replied.

There, in front of the hospital entrance, we all hugged each other, tears streaming.

From now on we would savor the small amount of time that was given to us.

***

I organized the acquisition of all the necessary amenities so we could nurse my grandfather at home. That included a hospital bed, a medical mattress to prevent pressure wounds, a wheelchair, and daily visits from a nurse. It was a lot of work, but if it meant that we could spend one last Christmas together, it was worth it.

On Christmas Eve, it was just the three of us.

Bobby Vinton's *My Christmas Prayer* sounded from the speakers in the decorated room. My grandfather closed his eyelids to savor the music. He said the song was magic. I wondered how much magic there could be in a house filled with despair and approaching death.

After a festive dinner, we huddled in front of the fireplace to watch two of his favorite movies, *Top Gun* and *Home Alone*. His eyes beamed with happiness.

***

To everyone's surprise, my grandfather exceeded his two weeks life expectancy. Bringing him home from the hospital had literally saved his life. But his condition remained precarious. I continued to spend as much time with him as possible while aiding my grandmother with the arduous tasks on hand: washing, feeding, making doctor appointments, shopping for groceries and medicines, and arranging necessities through the national health service--anything my grandmother couldn't manage on her own.

But, most importantly, I was trying to release my grandfather from the burden of his destiny by granting him moments of beauty through music and wine and cake and souvenirs. Or, perhaps, I created that beauty because I wasn't equipped to deal with the gray shroud of my grandfather's illness.

Both my grandmother and I deteriorated under the impact of our duties. Being confronted with powerlessness on a daily basis, my grandmother became rude to her husband and blamed him for her grief. Not wanting to cause any more suffering, I pent up my emotions, which resulted in frequent vomiting and fainting.

No one ever talked about how destructive it was to take care of someone in need of constant supervision. We couldn't complain about our weariness because the fate of the one we helped was worse than ours. It wasn't as beautiful an act as many believed. We couldn't possibly carry on like this. Yet how could we wish for our pain to end if that meant my grandfather's life would come to pass as well?

Contrary to my grandmother, I still had a home to escape to. Every night when I came back, frozen and exhausted, I would sit in the feeble light of the street lanterns pouring onto the sofa, and cry. And every night, Avalon sidled up next to me. Standing on his hind legs, he put both his paws around my neck, lurched his head forward and nuzzled his face against mine.

He would stay like this for as long as I needed him, as if he knew precisely what was happening and what I wanted him to do.

After a while, Avalon pulled away and I thought he'd leave, but then he licked away my tears, dozens of little kisses that eliminated the sorrow. His gentleness made me smile.

"Thank you for being here for me. I don't know what I'd do without you," I whispered to his ear.

Oftentimes, a call from my grandmother interrupted our intimacy. My grandfather had fallen out of bed and she couldn't haul him up.

My body bent against the punishing snow as I walked the same road over, each step leaving deeper marks of sadness. Sometimes I told myself that I'd done everything I could possibly do and I should start being selfish to survive. But when my grandfather broke into tears when I arrived, telling me how happy he was to see me, I once more felt that there was a poignancy in what I was doing.

But no matter how bad it got, it was okay, because I knew Avalon would be there when I came back. Our home was our shelter from the world, a far cry from the cavern of despair that was my grandparents' house. No matter how helpless I felt, going back to the life I had with Avalon made me feel more powerful than any king could derive from his riches. And no matter how profound my sorrow, when I looked into my cat's eyes, I thought, *I'm happy, because I have you.*

VAMPIRES

A few days after Christmas of the following year, I joined Pierre Lekeux and his wife Renata for dinner. A small group of other authors and filmmakers was invited as well. Though we scarcely knew each other, it felt like we were a group of close friends. We sat around the Christmas tree, ate the festive food Renata had prepared for us, drank champagne and wine in abundance, and exchanged gifts. Last year's struggles were nothing but a vague memory.

I could hardly believe how quickly life had changed again. It seemed almost miraculous that my grandfather, who hadn't been able to get out of bed for months, had suddenly started for the entrance hall, opened the front door for me, led me to the adjacent dining room, and stayed his independent self ever since. His health had literally improved overnight. A year ago, I would never have thought that I could spend yet another Christmas with my grandfather. It was something to be truly grateful for this evening.

As the night drew to a close, Pierre shared over liquor and cake that he wanted to play a vampire. "And you should write that movie for me," he added. "I have my own production company and there's already a partner in place. What do you think?"

"Vampires? Don't you think that's been done a bit too often?" I asked.

"Your voice is unique in Belgium. It's exactly what the genre needs. Why don't you think about it?"

"I will," I said, not convinced that this project was something I should be tackling.

That night, when I came home, I took the usual half hour to catch up with Avalon and give him his Christmas presents: a chicken Almo Nature meal sprinkled with fresh catnip, a big bowl of his favorite probiotic cat milk Viyo, and a huge assortment of toys.

As I watched Avalon devour his meal and milk, I was struck with an idea for the vampire story, and immediately took a pen and paper to jot down my thoughts.

I imagined how Pierre Lekeux's personality would mingle with vampirism--a 54-year-old vampire, suffering from a midlife crisis and arthritis, who seduces less attractive women to convince himself he's still desirable. And, of course, Avalon had to have a major part in the film.

Half an hour later Avalon's new catnip mice were shred to pieces, and the hallway was covered in drool. I was in bed, drinking a cup of tea and feverishly taking notes, when Avalon perched himself on my lap, his beard drenched.

I put my notes aside and took his face into my hands. "I have another Christmas present for you, my lion. I'm going to write a vampire film for you, a real feature film in which you will be one of the main stars."

Still high on catnip, Avalon didn't appear to register the information. He purred wildly and big bubbles of drool puddled onto my chest.

***

I called my new vampire story *A Good Man,* as the main character, Louis Caron, was a vegetarian, who fed the homeless, and was concerned with the ecological future of the planet. But his altruism had a sinister edge: he was a vampire. After hundreds of years, he still struggled with being good and being a killer.

Avalon's role in the script highlighted this dual nature. Originally, he was the cat of one of Louis Caron's victims. Being lonely, the woman didn't stop talking about her feline companion, and expressed her need to want only what was best for him. After feeding on her, Louis Caron granted her last wish by adopting Avalon. Through pampering her cat, he could convince himself of his good nature.

Later in the story, Louis Caron got a visit from Inspector Taglioni who interrogated him regarding his date's disappearance. He also searched for her cat and showed Louis a picture of Avalon.

"I haven't seen neither your girlfriend nor her cat," Louis said.

"You have a cat too? A white one."

"What makes you say that?"

"Your jacket is covered with white hairs."

The inspector went on to explain that Avalon's breed, the Turkish Van cat, was extremely rare in Belgium. No more than a handful of people had such a cat. Finding the pet would surely help to identify the killer.

This police interrogation set in motion a downward spiral in which Louis made a series of bad decisions in an attempt to escape imprisonment.

Avalon became a constant throughout the entire screenplay, and, of course, I *had* to turn him into a vampire kitty. Instead of drinking the blood of humans, he drank the blood of other cats.

I finished the first draft of the screenplay by April. The next months were spent attending fundraiser events, meeting with potential directors and producers, listening to their requirements, and making any requested script adjustments.

Then toward autumn, once principle photography was underway, castings were organized and we found a series of promising actors who fit the parts.

The producers announced that Avalon would be a general thread throughout the promotional trailer. This is how they envisioned it:

- Louis Caron sits on a couch lit by a fireplace. We don't see his face, just the back of his head.
- Avalon walks by an hourglass sitting on a bar. He descends, crosses the room in the dark, and mounts a sideboard with a book on it. The book contains an old picture serving as a bookmark.
- Flashback. Louis Caron reads on a bench by the lake. He pauses to watch a grandmother and her little girl approaching the water's edge. They make him smile. The yellow picture inside the open book on Louis' lap shows a woman in a ball gown.
- Back in the house, Avalon walks along the countertop and, with his tail, strokes a jar with a gold fish and a photo of an amorous couple in their thirties.

- Flashback. A meal between friends. The couple faces the camera and announces their future paternity. "You have always been like a father to me. Do you want to be the baby's godfather?"
- Avalon, now on the ground, passes a pile of women's attire.
- Flashback. Louis Caron hands a tramp a pile of clothes. "You want some clothes?" Louis Caron says. The tramp responds, "You are a good man."
- Ascending a small coffee table, Avalon licks the rim of a glass containing whisky.
- To the rhythm of gongs, the viewer is introduced to quick flashbacks of violent and strong scenes.
- Avalon approaches the couch where Louis Caron is seated. Rounding the corner, Avalon dives into a puddle of blood and climbs on top of the naked woman lying on Louis Caron's lap, leaving bloody paw prints on her body.
- The promotional trailer ends with a close-up of Louis Caron who rubs Avalon's head.

With such an important part, Avalon was well on his way to becoming Hollywood's next big thing.

MY ONLY CRIME IS LOVE

I'd never been the girl to fall in love easily. I didn't *get* romance. I was never crazy enough about a man that he occupied my thoughts day and night. I hadn't met someone who utterly infatuated me. Perhaps it was due to my belief that I wasn't good enough to have a boyfriend, or because of unrealistic expectations shaped by too many books and movies. While other women could date almost anyone who looked good or was friendly with them, I was rarely able to push my feelings past the friendship stage. Love equaled doubt--doubt in myself, and doubt in others.

I liked being alone. It was the only time I didn't feel judged. I craved that comfortable isolation so much that I'd even constructed my professional and personal life around it. Rather than doing a job that required social interaction, I'd write alone in a coffee shop. Rather than going to a bar, I'd prefer to read.

But most of all, when it came to love, I already felt accomplished. Avalon gave me a sense of belonging and stability. Looking at the lives of some friends who cheated on their partners and complained that they were nagged at, I felt blessed. And because I had all the love I needed, I didn't feel pressured to be different or better. I was finally at peace with myself. For the insecure and desperate girl I used to be, this was the most precious gift of all.

So when friends or family asked me about love, I joked about Avalon being the man of my life. I didn't need a real one. It was closer to the truth than they realized.

Avalon and I were happy in our little cocoon. A third party would only disrupt the bliss we had created for ourselves.

But then I did meet someone. And, ironically, Avalon was the reason I met my soon-to-be boyfriend.

Like all other life-changing events in my life, this one also happened during a film festival. On March 6, the Offscreen Film Festival opened with a reception and a screening of Guy Maddin's gangster movie *Keyhole*. The entire festival hall was adorned with movie set pieces. At the top of the stairs leading to the cellar bar, a prop from the Japanese ghost movie *Housu* caught my eye. It was an eccentric painting of a white fluffy cat bearing a striking resemblance to Avalon, except that it had vampire fangs, a humongous red mouth, and two glowing, yellow light bulbs as eyes.

The second I saw the canvas, I knew it was meant to be mine. Even before *Keyhole* started, I enquired with one of the organizers if it was possible to purchase the artwork. I wanted to be the first to ask the question, because I knew how quickly those props found a new owner. He agreed and we exchanged business cards so we could make arrangements after the festival.

Three days later, I returned to Offscreen with a friend to watch the movies *Next Of Kin* and *Death Weekend*. After the first film, which was about a haunted home for the elderly, we headed downstairs to the cellar bar. The organizer, Gilles, with whom I arranged to purchase the cat painting, immediately came over to talk to us. When it was time to see *Death Weekend*, my friend Frank said, "I'm actually more in the mood to carry on my conversation with Gilles. Let's stay here instead of watching the film."

Frank could be a real groupie with movie people, and once Gilles had started talking about his job as a movie poster designer, I knew that chances of getting Frank out of there were slim.

"No problem, " I said." I can go alone."

"Can't I convince you to stay?" Frank pleaded. "I'll make sure I'll find that film so you don't have to miss it."

After some insisting, I agreed.

For the next four hours, the three of us talked about our respective careers and favorite movie monsters. It was fun to see how much Gilles and I had in common. We were both artists, loved horror movies, respected animals, and swore by a vegetarian lifestyle.

Gilles' interest in me was obvious to many. I, on the other hand, was oblivious. Romance wasn't on my mind. It wasn't conscious. It was merely a subconscious out-of-my-league feeling I didn't analyze. Surely he would soon realize I wasn't talented, established, and interesting enough to be considered his girl. My sense of self-worth relied on Avalon, and when confronted with people, not even the sweetest words could give me assurance.

Over the next three weeks, I returned to Offscreen several times, and every night Gilles and I talked about our mutual passion for movies and animals. On the days I wasn't there, he emailed to say how much he enjoyed our conversation.

Still, despite the strong first impression and the many things we had in common, I immediately slotted Gilles into the friends-category. He was an interesting connection. Nothing more. I knew from the first night we met that he was somebody I wanted to be friends with. Anything more than that represented a challenge I might not be up to.

The first time he asked me out, I regarded our date as nothing more than a formal meeting to collect the *Housu* painting.

The next time we saw each other was at a reception party from the Japanese embassy. The sole purpose of Gilles' presence was to see me, but thinking he was there for business, I paid him no mind the entire evening.

Gilles almost gave up on me that day. He decided to give it one more try and asked if I could get tickets for a film festival where I had a gig. I could, so off we went to a 3D screening of Takashi Shimuzu's *Rabitto Horâ*.

Dinner was next, and throughout the days that followed, we phoned and emailed on a daily basis.

For our next "date" we opted for an exhibition of Stanley Kubrick's photography, and dinner in an Italian restaurant.

"I never told you this, but I've actually known you for almost twenty years," Gilles told me afterwards in a bar. "I've seen you host Q&A sessions at the Brussels International Fantastic Film Festival, and I wondered who you were."

"But we've never spoken to each other before, right?"

"You were with your boyfriend. You were taken."

For the first time, it dawned on me that Gilles had started to fall in love with me. Obviously I liked him too; I was just the last one to realize. My experience was that the men I was interested in didn't like me back, so as soon as I'd noticed Gilles' qualities, I unconsciously blocked my feelings to protect myself.

"I checked out a couple of your interviews online," Gilles said. "I remember a journalist asking what supernatural talent you'd want to possess. Most people would reply flying or becoming invisible. But you said you'd want to be able to cure your cat and talk to him. When I read that, I knew you were special."

He looked at me tenderly and closed his hand over mine.

I was dumbstruck, so taken off balance by the turn of events that I was unable to utter another word. Gilles broke the silence by kissing me.

As our evening drew to a close, he walked me back to the train station.

"Would you like to stay tonight?" he asked.

"I can't. I have to feed my cat."

"I'm sure he can survive a night without food, can't he?"

"Survive, yes. But he would be miserable, and I don't want that."

"Your cat really means a lot to you, doesn't it?"

"More than anything."

***

That night, Avalon greeted me with all his usual fervor. He pinned himself to me, and rubbed his whole face vigorously against my cheeks as if we'd been apart for weeks.

However, something was different. Like someone who had just cheated on her husband, I was unable to look him in the eye.

Little did I know that Avalon's possessiveness still lay dormant. My cat was about to do everything in his power to keep his winning position.

MEET THE CAT

Most men are anxious to meet their new girlfriend's parents. Will they be accepted into the family? My family didn't concern Gilles, though. After all the stories he'd heard about Avalon, he was worried about getting my cat's approval.

At first I didn't realize what was going on. After a few weeks of Gilles making excuses not to come to my place, I started to doubt our relationship. I didn't want to leave Avalon alone for too long, and I refused to spend several nights a week out. When I questioned him about why he avoided my apartment, he blushed and said, "I'm afraid of what your cat might think of me."

"My cat's opinion matters to you? Why?"

"What if he hates me? I know how important Avalon is to you. You might change your mind about me if Avalon doesn't give his approval."

"You'll have to meet him eventually."

***

Days before his first confrontation with Avalon, Gilles was conspicuously ill at ease. And when the moment of truth arrived, Avalon did nothing to allay the situation. Only minutes after Gilles entered, a putrid waft spread throughout the apartment. Avalon had used his litter box and charged from the room, belting out a rumbling growl. He bounced from wall to wall before leapfrogging on the backrest of the sofa, right behind Gilles.

Not expecting any of this, Gilles startled.

Letting out another, even louder growl, Avalon sprinted back into the air, *flying* above the living room table, and finally landing on the TV set in front of us. From there, he took another leap onto the wall where, like a koala, he climbed toward the ceiling. He stayed there for several seconds, let out a new roar, hopped off, then galloped to the bedroom.

In the wild, lions growl for several reasons--to point out their territory, to intimidate rivals, and to enforce a relationship. It would be easy to interpret this demeanor according to the laws of nature.

"Am I the cause of this behavior?" he asked.

"No, this is normal."

"Normal?"

"Yeah, it's Avalon's typical post-litterbox behavior. Nothing to worry about."

"If this is normal, then how will he react if he becomes jealous of me?"

"Let's not ruin the mood, shall we?"

***

Against all expectations, however, Avalon behaved. He wasn't nearly as affectionate as when he was alone with me, but he didn't cause havoc either. Keeping an eye on us from a distance while Gilles and I had dinner in front of a movie, Avalon refused any form of closeness as if he communicated, *It's either him or me.* Afterwards he refused to come to bed with me, and slept on the sofa like an angered spouse wanting to make a point.

Around three o'clock that night, Avalon was fed up with the strange man in *his* bed. He plonked his rear down on Gilles' pillow, complaining fretfully in his ear while tapping him on the face.

After nearly an hour of incessant wailing and poking, more drastic measures were required. The new solution: pushing Gilles out of bed.

Avalon succeeded.

Climbing back under the covers wasn't an option. Unable to sleep, Gilles got up. "I guess I didn't pass the test."

"Give Avalon some time. Maybe he was just irked because you took his side of the bed."

But Gilles had already understood that this wasn't going to be a one-time event.

For several minutes, Gilles and Avalon sized each other up. Then Gilles said, "I'd better leave the two of you alone now. It's clearly what the little guy wants."

I swear I could see Avalon smirking when Gilles put on his jacket and left.

Instantly, Avalon leapt onto me, and compensated for the evening before. He entered a kiss-induced trance. An ecstatic look brightened his face and clearly he was in nirvana. He'd reached the holy land.

This cat was all about exclusivity, and when granted that exclusivity, his love was immense.

"Are you really that happy that Gilles is gone?"

In reply, Avalon looked at me with swoony eyes and purred loudly, then swatted out his paw to urge me to continue to pet him, which I did.

A phone call interrupted our tender moment. It was Gilles.

"There won't be any train to Brussels for hours," he said. "Is it okay if I come back to your place for a while?"

"Of course." His return would offend Avalon, but I couldn't possibly leave Gilles outside in the rain for several hours.

As soon as Gilles appeared at the front door, Avalon's pupils widened to a pitch black.

Let's see who's the boss here, he seemed to be thinking.

Being a cat of action, Avalon went through his usual attention-seeking routine: making a selection of irritating noises, scratching the wallpaper, and pushing objects to the ground.

When that didn't work, Avalon opened Gilles' overnight bag and threw out a piece of clothing. His eyes so dark and evil they could be gateways to hell, Avalon stared at his adversary and waited for a reaction. He then pulled out a box of gel wax. Again, he looked up at Gilles to make sure he understood that all this bungling was meant to get a message across. A third object followed, then a fourth, a fifth, a sixth, until there was nothing.

Hell-bent on winning the game, Avalon took Gilles' coat in his mouth and towed it toward the front door. There, he used his right paw to tap the keys hanging from the wooden doorframe.

Avalon's message couldn't be any clearer: there was room for only one man in my life. A feline one.

MUTUAL DEPENDENCY

I had often read that cats have no sense of time. They aren't supposed to know if you're gone for only one minute or several hours. I didn't believe this. Avalon might have been incapable of measuring the number of minutes and hours, but he definitely behaved differently if I'd been away for one hour or an entire day. Three to four hours was about the longest he could stand. Longer than that and Avalon cried his lungs out on my return.

Scientists believe that when the cat owners leave and don't return, the cats think that predators devoured them. That's supposedly why cats are so happy to see you when you come back. Was this also the reason why Avalon always sat in front of the window, waiting impatiently for me to come home? It didn't matter at what time of day I arrived, if it was at two in the afternoon or five in the morning. Avalon was there, waiting. His ability to predict my homecoming was infallibly precise.

Most pets have a sense of smell much greater than that of any human being. Was it possible that Avalon caught my scent when I was inside a car? I read somewhere that researchers concocted an odor in a lab and taught a bloodhound to react to it. They took the hound to the bottom of Manhattan Island, while others on the team traveled thirteen miles away. At the top of Manhattan, at a prearranged time, the researchers saturated a cloth with the laboratory-brewed smell, and waved the cloth in the air. Less than a minute later, the hound reacted to the scent, even though air currents must have widely dispersed the molecules into a miasma of uncountable other smells.

Avalon was no bloodhound, but he knew which car I was in, even though that car was rarely the same. Though he couldn't see me, at the instant the car turned the street he erupted out of listless depression into pure delight.

However, I didn't realize how deep-seated Avalon's abandonment phobia was until I went on vacation. Things couldn't have been worse if I'd moved out forever. My dad and his wife, Dominique, took good care of Avalon, playing with him and feeding his favorite meals in abundance, but none of that mattered if the two of us weren't breathing the same air.

I had left as little as possible to chance, preparing a note with lengthy instructions as if I had left a critically ill infant in their care.

FOOD: Avalon eats twice a day. The measuring cup is inside the bag. Please clean his food dish between each meal.

MEDICATION: Twice daily, mix half a pill of Felimazole with half a box of his favorite cat food brand, Almo Nature. Avoid crushing the pill as this is toxic.

WATER: Avalon has two water bowls, one in the hallway and one in the bedroom. Both have to be cleaned and filled daily.

CAT MILK: Avalon appreciates his cat milk. He's particularly crazy about the probiotic drink Viyo. You may give him one sachet a day.

LITTER BOXES: Both litter boxes have to be cleaned out daily.

WINDOWS AND DOORS: Windows and doors must remain closed. Avalon is not used to the outside, so he might get lost. Don't leave windows ajar either when you're not there, because Avalon could get stuck and choke. The kitchen door should be locked too as Avalon can, and will, open the door to the fridge. The bedroom door, however, should be open at all times, because Avalon likes to sleep in bed.

PLAY: Avalon will appreciate a good twenty minutes of daily playtime. The fishing rod is his absolute favorite. Catnip toys are a close second. The fishing rod can be found in the drawer of the living room table. There are at least thirty catnip toys in the cardboard box next to the sofa.

LOVE: And most importantly: Give Avalon lots of love. He may be able to live several days without food, water, and play, but he's unable to live a single day without being loved. If you think you've given him enough affection, then give him some more.

During my stay abroad, I asked for daily news reports about Avalon and each time my dad texted me, "He's fine. No need to worry."

Despite his reassurances, I couldn't stop fretting about Avalon. What on earth had come over me to leave such a dependent cat alone for a week? How would he cope with my absence? What if a burglar chased him out the house and, unable to find his way back home, Avalon would be lost to me forever? What if he died suddenly and I couldn't be there for him?

On my return, when I opened the door to my building foyer, I was welcomed to a pathetic mournful wail. As soon as I entered my flat, Avalon jumped into my arms and held on to me as if his life depended on it. Even though he had been well cared for, he had transformed into a pitiful, scrawny cat with a rough coat and dull eyes.

After a few minutes, I tried to put him back on the floor, but he wouldn't let go of me. He clung to me for five hours straight, the way a shipwreck survivor clings to a piece of floating wood.

Because Avalon was as lost without me as a diabetic without insulin, it became increasingly difficult to be a few hours away without feeling guilty.

But I also noticed how easy it was to make Avalon's eyes light up with delight. I never knew someone could be this overjoyed just by being with me. This realization gave me moments of sheer bliss. At the same time, it impressed on me a sense of responsibility, knowing that the spark in his eyes could easily be disabled if I didn't give in to that dependency.

Avalon came with limitations. I dreamed about writing in sunny locations and attending film festivals all over the world, but that fantasy had to be put on hold as long as Avalon was with me. Like any relationship, this one had its costs. I came to accept the price and balance it against the obvious advantages. I accepted Avalon with all the constraints he brought with him, and even loved him all the more for it.

***

AVALON

Gilles had more trouble accepting Avalon's impositions. After each sleepover at Gilles', no matter how scarce they were, Avalon looked gaunt, as if my nightly absence meant that I was never to return. Because Avalon was so ill-equipped to deal with solitude, Gilles made a continuous effort to sleep at my place so that my cat didn't have to be alone at night.

Avalon did not respect the effort. Convinced that exclusive love was the highest good in this world, Avalon did everything in his power to communicate that Gilles wasn't welcome. No matter how I tried to distract, cajole, or plead with him, he mewed frantically all night long and scampered around the apartment like a tornado, making a maximum of DVDs and shoe boxes fall to the ground, preferably with as much noise as possible.

But once Gilles left, everything returned to normal.

After a couple of months, the question of moving in with my boyfriend surfaced.

The answer was, no.

I wanted Avalon's last years of his life to be peaceful, and moving in with a man and his two cats would guarantee the opposite.

Ideally, for Avalon's wellbeing, I should have left Gilles. Of course, no matter how enamored I was with my cat that would have been irrational.

So when no solution turned out to be convenient, I made a decision that was equally insane. It was time to start seeing Gilles less often, at least for the time being.

Many were shocked that I put my human relationship second to my cat. It was a battle in which I knew I'd never gain any ground. Having never experienced such an all-consuming connection with an animal, most people didn't comprehend it.

They could only compare my situation with their own experiences and standards.

I felt it would have been unfair to deny Avalon's needs considering everything he meant to me. He may not have been my family or my boyfriend, but he was my companion, and he brought more happiness, stability, and comfort than anyone else I had known.

Gilles, on the other hand, still had to earn my trust. After all, I'd only known him for a few months. There was no guarantee his image of me wouldn't be bruised one day and that he wouldn't start to ask more of me than I could give. Deep down, I expected Gilles to be as demanding as everyone else.

However, there was a selfish side to my decision, too. I was as attached to our exclusivity as Avalon. Sharing my cat with someone else would inevitably change our relationship. On those evenings where Gilles stayed over at my place, Avalon behaved like a regular cat; the hours of pure tenderness were only meant for when we were alone together.

"Avalon's not distant with you when I'm here," Gilles said when I expressed my concerns. "He follows you around all the time. He never leaves your side."

"That's true. But still, he's not as stodgy as when he's alone with me."

"Honestly, I don't want to know what that must be like. The two of you always look at each other with melting adoration. You never look at me that way."

There was definitely truth in that, but I didn't want to risk losing part of Avalon's affection. So if moving in with Gilles meant that Avalon and I would be less close, my mind was made up. In fact, it made me realize that the bond I shared with Avalon was one out of a million, and that it had an intensity that I would never experience again. I wanted to indulge in our infatuation for as long as I could.

When it came to love, it was Avalon against the rest of the world. The human population would always be on the losing side of a never-ending tenderness for my cat.

YOU SMELL LIKE LOVE

"Don't tell me how to say my lines," said Pierre Lekeux to *A Good Man* director Steve De Roover. "I'm a brilliant actor."

"I'm not saying you aren't," Steve tried cautiously. "I would just like you to try another approach for that one line. It would sound much better if mumbled, a fleeting thought. Matthias' character doesn't hear you, remember?"

"That's because you have no idea what your film is about," Pierre spit back.

And on it went, both sounding as recriminatory as the other. The more the discussion went on, the more they sounded like two people using phrasebooks to say things neither understood. It didn't matter if someone asked for pizza or another shooting angle, for Pierre it translated as, "Everyone conspires to fire me."

I once read that eighty percent of people in the movie business show signs of schizophrenia. It was only the first day of principle photography on *A Good Man*, but the truth of that saying was already starting to show.

Refusing to bear witness to Pierre's paranoia and fantasies of grandeur, I left the bar where they were shooting the film, and sat down at the terrace where some of the crew members were resting.

The director scurried out the bar as well, his hands lifted in despair. As he sat down at the table next to mine, he said, "He doesn't listen to me. I'm the director, and he just ...doesn't ... listen ... to me. I don't mind giving an actor freedom, but he doesn't get the character. Have you seen the rushes from this morning, the ones in the park?"

I shook my head.

"He looks at those kids as if he's a pedophile. I can't use that in the film."

As the director went on about his issues, my cell phone rang. It was my grandmother.

"Grandma? Is everything okay?"

"Your grandfather... He's unwell. The doctor is here now. They're going to bring him to the hospital."

I left the set immediately.

***

It was nudging July when the first rays of sunshine of the year brightened the streets. A couple of friends had invited Gilles and me to a birthday dinner. We settled on a Thai restaurant that offered alfresco seating. Our sidewalk table was shaded, with a view of the piazza. The smell of the fresh summer air mingled with the aromas of lemongrass, garlic, and Thai basil. It had been a long winter, but now that summer had finally kicked in, we all wanted to get the most out of it.

But I was feeling conflicted. The production of *A Good Man* had come to a halt when the director was fired. I feared that

Avalon would never play the special part I wrote for him if the shooting didn't pick up any time soon.

While I toasted to a beautiful evening in the still summer air, my thoughts were also with my grandfather and the day we'd spent together. Though he was back home from the hospital, he was bed-bound, continuously rattling, coughing, and gasping for air.

Being confronted with how frail life could be, I was also reminded to live life to the fullest. After all, my grandfather had been the one to teach me about the pleasures of vacations, good food, wine, and sun, but not without working hard and giving the best of myself at all times. For tonight, at least, I wanted to continue that legacy. If he couldn't enjoy life anymore, then I would do it for him, because I knew he would have wanted me to. So, for a few hours, I tried to live in the moment, relishing the food and the sun he used to appreciate so much.

But despite my positivity, I was anxious about my grandfather's failing health. It was a few minutes to eleven when my cell phone announced a new message. I jumped out of my seat. A message this late could never be good news.

"What is it?" Gilles asked.

I looked at the screen and relaxed. "Only the receipt of a text message I sent two weeks ago. The guy must have been on vacation, I guess."

"Do you realize how high you jumped when you heard that message?"

"I suppose I'm a little on edge."

"Sooner or later you *will* get that dreaded phone call. You know that, don't you?"

My cell phone rang again, this time with a phone number I didn't know. A female voice asked, "Are you Vanessa?"

"Yes."

"I'm from Family Care, the organization that's keeping your grandmother company tonight," the voice said. "I'm calling to inform you that your grandfather, Mr. Joseph Janssens, died at two minutes before eleven tonight."

My legs began to buckle.

"I'm so sorry for your loss. Do you want to talk to your grandmother?"

I managed a small, "Yes."

My grandmother was sobbing at the other end of the line. A heartbreaking sound.

"I'm coming over," I told her.

"You don't have to. Enjoy your evening with Gilles."

"I'm not going to leave you alone tonight," I said. "I'll be there as quickly as I can."

We borrowed a friend's car and half an hour later, we were on our way to my grandmother's. I spent the night at her place.

***

For the next two weeks I dealt with funeral home directors, notaries, bank clerks, insurance brokers, and priests. My grandmother was too confused to deal with them on her own. Because of that, I spent long stretches of time away from home. For Avalon, this was a disaster. Every time, on seeing me put on my coat and take my handbag, Avalon reacted with a piercing *Me-oooow* that strummed a fearful twang in my stomach. With panic showing in his eyes, he threw himself in front of the door, blocking my exit.

"I don't really have the choice now, baby lion," I told him. "My grandmother is all alone now, and I need to help her. I *promise* it will only take a couple of weeks, maybe even days, before I'm all yours again."

Avalon picked up on my emotions, and he calmed down. But as soon as my hand touched the doorknob, Avalon's panic flared back in full force. With as much drama as only Donald Duck could muster, he threw himself in front of the door to prevent me from leaving. I gave him a gentle nudge, and shut the door behind me, not knowing what else I could do.

Avalon never got used to us being apart, but even more so than in the past. He reacted differently to my absence, clingier than ever.

I wondered if his behavior had anything to do with his health. Sometime during the end of the winter I had noticed several changes in Avalon that had seemingly happened overnight and that had moved him out of middle age and into retirement.

Ever so quietly he was losing muscle mass in his lumbar paravertebral area, typical for felines with thyroid disease. I initially only felt it when I ran my hand over his back, but after a few months, there was no denying how bony he had become. His once lustrous fur had gradually worn down to sticky tangles. His eyesight had become fuzzy. Because he was shedding fur in large quantities, he gawked out hairballs as if he was trying to beat a world record.

Another change was his need for fresh air. Whenever I opened a window, he would stick his head out and hold his snout in the breeze, sniffing the air like a lion spotting the scent of an antelope.

After a couple of weeks, however, he could no longer jump onto the windowsill himself. He either stumbled off and fell, or found himself awkwardly stuck.

From then on, he looked up at me from under the perch of his favorite kitchen window and implored me to haul him up. I slapped my hands. "Come on, Avalon. I know you can do it." But he was immobilized. I took him in my arms and positioned him onto the desired spot.

Avalon was beginning to slow down in other ways too. He still had his bursts of unbridled, adrenaline-pumped energy, especially when an unwanted human entered the house, but mostly he was content to snooze at my side most of the day. The effect of aging was undeniable.

As soon as I noticed these changes, I took him to Dr. Henri for another round of blood-works. Despite the wide variety of symptoms, he assured me that there was nothing to worry about and that the disease was under control. Avalon had been on the low iodine Hill's Prescription Diet y/d for several months now and, apparently, this had even better effects on his hyperthyroidism than his previous hormone treatments.

I pleaded with him to check for other possible conditions, which he did, but he maintained his diagnosis: Avalon was perfectly healthy.

"Your cat looks fine. Look how energetic he is," Gilles confirmed. "I'm sure you're only imagining this because you're so worried."

Still, the nagging feeling of something being wrong remained and I feared that our days together were limited.

In the book *The Hour of Our Deaths*, Philippe Ariès wrote that the essential characteristic of death, even if sudden or accidental, is that it "gives advance warning of its arrival" and that "only the dying man can tell how much time he has left." Two weeks before he passed, my grandfather said he felt his life was coming to an end. I asked why he said that, if he was in pain or was feeling discomfort somehow. "Not at all. I can just feel it," he said.

I believed that Avalon was now communicating this knowledge to me as well. It wouldn't be the first time I knew something was wrong with him before it actually happened. Avalon may not have sprouted from my body, but he had awakened in me a tenderness that probably equaled having a child of my own. His wellbeing was my priority and all I wanted was to protect this cat.

In the worst case, I hoped that when the time came, I could be there for him, holding him in my arms. I didn't want him to be alone in those moments.

I didn't allow myself much time to pursue that line of thinking. It was too hard. I knew I couldn't control the way this was going to unfold, and there was little point in torturing myself with different possible scenarios.

I didn't want to give up my precious time with my cat, and I wanted to curtail any activity that kept me away from him. But there was still my grandmother who needed my help. So every evening, on my way back home, I accelerated my step in the hopes of being with Avalon a little sooner.

On my return, he powered into my arms with a force that almost knocked me down. I sank to the floor, and he burrowed his head into my neck as hard as he could.

Most of the time, though, I was so tired from grappling with life's grim duties that I fell asleep almost immediately. Avalon hugged me in bed, but all I could do was curl up and keep my arm around him.

In the weeks following my grandfather's passing, I suffered recurring nightmares in which Avalon was in danger. They were all about the same subject. A natural disaster, such as a gargantuan flood or fire, menaced my life, and all I could think of was to get back to my apartment to save my cat. Most of the time my grandparents were with me, but they were only an encumbrance. "What are you doing? We have to get out of here," my grandmother shouted. With all her might, she tried to keep me inside the car while I watched the flood or fire approach our apartment where Avalon hid.

"Let go of me," I screamed. "Avalon is alone in there. I have to save him."

"You can't risk your life for a cat," my grandmother said, still tugging at my arm.

"He's more than *just* a cat."

Danger was approaching fast. Only a few more minutes were left to get Avalon out of there.

I broke free and ran off in the direction of my apartment while the water rushed closer. Behind me, a large gulf swallowed my grandparents' car. Just when I opened the front door to my apartment, the water got to me as well.

I was never able to save my cat.

Each time, I woke up with a deep feeling of foreboding. I hugged Avalon as close to me as I could.

***

As the days passed, the feeling of dread grew. Ever increasingly, I needed to be with Avalon to make sure he was safe. After two weeks of constantly caring for my grandmother, I couldn't stand to be away from Avalon anymore. I *had* to be with him.

On Friday, I helped my grandmother with duties in the morning and, to great opposition, went home after lunch. My sister Jennifer, too, called that day to ask if she could come over in the evening. I hadn't seen her in over a month, but as soon as the idea of being separated from Avalon surfaced, tears streamed down my face.

"I don't know what's come over me," I said. "All I can think of is that something bad is going to happen to Avalon and I need to be with him."

"You've been under a lot of pressure lately. I think it's normal that you worry so much about him with all that's happened."

"Is it okay if we see each other some other time? I really need to be alone with him."

"No problem. I know how much the two of you need each other."

For the rest of the day, Avalon and I didn't leave each other's side. In the afternoon, I worked from home, filling in my taxes while Avalon sat in the sofa next to me.

In the evening, I went to bed early. With the movie *The Unborn* playing in the background, I worked on a new supernatural novel of suspense, set in an accursed village. Something bad happens to the townspeople each time one of the local cats dies. Of course, my new novel held a major part for Avalon.

As I imagined his role in the story, Avalon lay next to me on the bed, keeping his gaze glued on me.

He sensed my need for affection and, of course, he made himself available. All I had to do was say his name, and he stood up immediately and caressed his head against my cheeks. His perpetual readiness for love was endearing.

This was how life was supposed to be--just the two of us, Avalon and me. We had really missed that over the past few weeks.

Later that night, he stretched out beside me and slid his snout beneath my nose. I wish I could have stopped time at that very moment. I wanted to be Bill Murray in *Groundhog Day*, living the same day over and over.

Lying there with him, I couldn't help thinking of that night on the streets when he stopped in his tracks when he first saw me and decided to follow me home. Twelve years later, we were more inseparable than ever. I thought about his difficult childhood, about all the shredded walls and plundered refrigerators, about his vomit sessions on the guinea pig, and his pangs of jealousy that had driven everyone to distraction. But I also thought about our many cheek-to-jowl dances with the stereo blaring Kenji Kawai's soundtrack for the movie he was named after, and about all the moments of feline-human tenderness that outclassed any of the great romance novels I had read.

I inhaled the smell of the fur of his neck--a mix between fresh laundry and cupcakes--and I tried to imprint his odor into my memory.

I told him, "You smell like love."

We fell asleep together, side by side, my arm draped across his back.

It was to be our last night together.

SOULMATES

Saturday started perfectly with Avalon's long-stretched ritual of smooches in bed. I'd only just opened my eyes, awake yet half asleep, when Avalon, who snoozed at my feet, sensed the variation in my breathing, and got up to greet me with face licks and head bumps.

In the past, I used to run my hand over his back before turning to catch a few additional minutes of sleep. Since Avalon had started to dominate my worries, I made a conscious effort to stay awake and focus my attention on him.

When I got out of bed, Avalon still clung to me like duct tape. In the kitchen, I fetched him a bowl of kibble and gave him some fresh water, but when I started across the corridor, saying, "Qui veut manger?" he didn't respond with his usual, "Moi. Moi. Moi." Instead, he waited for me on the sofa, pawing the cushions impatiently, which he did when he needed me.

I couldn't refuse him such a tender supplication.

I had promised my grandmother to come over at noon and help her with the administration I failed to do the day before, but Avalon was so dependent on me that day that I called to cancel.

The only thing I wanted was to spend time with the cat I had hardly seen over the past few weeks.

Later that day, in the evening, Gilles would come over to spend the night. There were still a few things to do beforehand, such as cleaning up the apartment and doing groceries, and I planned on doing this first so that nothing or no one could separate me from Avalon later on.

As soon as I neared the front door to go get groceries, Avalon blocked my exit, wailing like a siren as if he'd never see me again if I dared to leave the house.

I kneeled down and caressed his head. "I'll be back before you know it," I told him.

Still, he pleaded for me to stay.

I gave him a peck on the nose and left.

When I came home forty-five minutes later, Avalon's breakfast was all over the bedroom, including on the walls. Usually, his vomiting was controlled--on a self-selected spot and never that much. Certainly not on the walls.

My first reaction was to consult Google to see if the vomiting could have anything to do with the heat wave of the past few days, even if today was cooler.

While I sat down in the living room behind my computer, Avalon kept staring at me from within the bedroom.

"Why are you so far from me?" I asked him.

Hearing my voice should have been enough to bring him over, but he didn't budge. His gaze stayed glued on me; he never once looked away.

"Why don't you come sit with me?" I asked again, in vain.

We may have been only one room away from each other, but for our standards it was miles. He was probably still feeling unwell and had searched out the coolest spot in the apartment, next to the ajar window.

When I approached, I expected him to get up and greet me. Instead, he kept staring at me, his eyes locked on mine, searching for answers to questions that hadn't been asked. As I crouched beside him, he mewed in a way I hadn't heard before. He wanted to communicate something. But what?

"What are you trying to tell me, my lion? Are you ill? Do you want me to call the vet?"

He answered with a set of long, plaintive meows.

Avalon kept calm and immobile and just tried to communicate. Something about his behavior made me feel uncomfortable. Basically, he had just vomited and didn't immediately come over to me when called. Nothing to be anxious about, really. However, Avalon and I had developed such a strong connection over the years that we could easily pick up on each other's thoughts. And these thoughts spurred me to call the veterinarian--immediately. Knowing Avalon's fear of vets and his previous pleas to never take him there again, I knew that this time something was going on that couldn't wait.

I took his head between my hands, and touched his forehead with my lips. His eyes softly closed as he treasured the kiss.

Then I got up, sat down on the bed next to him, and called the nearby veterinary clinic. The receptionist told me that one of their vets would be there in one or two hours. Sooner was impossible. It was office hours and all their veterinarians were busy. Without a car, I didn't have any other choice than to wait.

I put down the phone and lay next to him. He put his paws over my hands and pushed them against my flesh. Whenever I moved, he pulled me closer to him, wanting me as near as possible. I ran my other hand across his long, soft fur and brought my face closer to him. That's when I realized he didn't have any control over his saliva.

Shocked, I backed away, reaching for my phone. This time I called my father's wife, Dominique, to ask her if she could offer me a ride to the veterinary clinic. She agreed.

In the time it took to call Dominique, Avalon had moved closer to the open window and was now panting and gasping for air.

I took him into my arms. The saliva trickling from his mouth had turned into thick white mucus.

"Everything will be all right, my lion. I'll never let anything happen to you. You're safe. I'm here." I believed I had that power.

For the first time in his life, he didn't fight me when I loaded him into his carrier. I couldn't begin to imagine what had caused this sudden emergency.

With Avalon still in his carrier, I waited for Dominique downstairs on the boardwalk in front of our apartment. Minutes later, she picked us up and we were on our way to the clinic.

Inside the car, I kept Avalon's carrier on my lap. I opened it just enough to stick my hand in, and Avalon nuzzled against it in desperation. I continued talking to him in a soft, reassuring voice, "The vet is going to cure you, my lion. You'll be home in no time."

***

The waiting room was full to the brim. People of all ages were waiting wide-eyed over their pet's fate. People were trying small talk. "Is that a cat in there?" "How old is he?" "Why are you here?"

Dominique and I told them what happened, that he was probably about fifteen years old, and that I was intent on pushing him over the brink of twenty. Meanwhile, I caressed Avalon's forehead and body, quietly telling him that he was going to be okay.

Time inside the waiting room was heavy with foreboding, progressing slower than the pace at which Avalon was regressing. Panting and drooling, he could now hardly muster the force to lift his head.

I asked for urgent assistance, and the vet only needed to cast a glance at Avalon to realize it was a matter of life and death.

Without hesitation we were taken into the exam room. The vet took Avalon out of his pet carrier and onto the examination table. He peered into his eyes, and opened his mouth to look inside. "Has he been poisoned?" he asked.

"I don't think so."

"His abdomen's swollen and his mouth is red from irritation. Those are signs of poisoning."

"I have no idea what could've caused a poisoning. He never leaves the apartment."

The veterinarian pressed a stethoscope against various parts of Avalon's sides and chest.

"His blood pressure is over eighteen. That's way too high for a cat. We'll have to get that blood pressure down before we can do anything else, otherwise he might risk a heart attack from stress," the vet said. "Let me give him an injection to help him with that. Can you keep him still?"

I crossed my arms over Avalon's body while he was lying on the examination table, more to give comfort than to restrain him. No matter how much Avalon hated vets and how aggressive he'd been with them in the past, this time he didn't stir. He didn't so much as twitch a muscle.

Meanwhile, the vet took a medicine out of the large white cupboard near the door and prepared for the injection.

With Avalon's head cemented against my belly and his front paws crossed around my waist, the vet inserted the needle. Avalon held onto me, pushing hard against my body, seeking protection, as if his life depended on it. He was counting on me to help him, but for the first time in my life, I didn't know if I would be able to do that.

"It's for your own good, my baby," I said. "The vet is helping you get better. You'll soon be able to go home with me."

I was surprisingly calm. I didn't want to distress Avalon with my tears while he struggled to breathe. But inside, the fear burned me up. There's nothing worse than seeing the one you love suffer in agony, fighting for his life and counting on you to save him.

"Can you go outside for a minute?" the vet asked. "I'd like to do an x-ray of Avalon's chest. There might be water in there that prevents him from breathing normally."

I gave Avalon a comforting kiss and left the room. When I returned less than a minute later, the x-rays were already up on the viewer.

"As I had feared, the x-rays show an accumulation of fluid in Avalon's chest, but not enough to provide any clues to the cause of his breathing difficulties. There must be something else," the vet said. "I'm afraid that doing any more examinations might cause his blood pressure to rise. The best thing we can do for now is to let him rest in the oxygen tank."

As he prepared the tank, I took Avalon back into my arms. He felt heavier than usual.

"You can put him in now," the vet said when he was ready.

AVALON

I whisked Avalon into the oxygen tank and the vet gave him an infusion.

With the extra hit of oxygen, Avalon turned aggressive for the first time today. He clawed at his vet. As a result, he earned a shot of valium.

"That's all we can do for now," he said. "I suggest you go home and we'll call you later to keep you informed."

"There's no way I'm going to leave Avalon alone here."

"Avalon will have to stay here for several hours, maybe even all day. There's nothing you can do. You can't even touch him when he's inside the oxygen tank."

Dominique had been waiting for me and spoke up. "Let's just go home. We can come back later." .

"You can go home, but I'm not going to leave him," I said. There was nothing they could say to convince me otherwise.

"The clinic will be closing this afternoon because we'll be starting our house visits. No one will be here. You can't stay."

I imagined Avalon being all by himself in this abandoned clinic, afraid and struggling for his life. Considering his state, I wasn't even sure I was going to see him alive again if I left. "We'll have to find an agreement, because I'm not leaving my cat alone."

When he realized I wasn't going to budge, he let me stay.

Half an hour later, Avalon still held his own, resting with an intravenous drip in his front limb. The vet announced he wanted to check Avalon's heart with a cat scan. I lifted him out of the oxygen tank and held him in my arms, pressing his body against me so I could feel his warmth. He was listless and hardly breathed.

"He's only numb with valium," the vet assured me.

As I placed him in front of the cat scan, I said in a low voice, "You have to fight to get better, my little baby lion. Please, *please,* stay with me and fight, because I can't live without you. I really *can't* live without you."

He offered nothing more than a blank stare, probably unaware of what I said.

Despite my best efforts, tears rolled down my face and splashed onto his.

After scanning Avalon's heart and examining the results, the vet called his colleague for a second opinion. His partner looked at the scans, grimacing. The results were obviously anything but positive.

"Everything black here, is the heart muscle," he said. "As you can see, there's a lot of it. And this little spot is what's left of his heart. It's so overgrown with muscle that it doesn't have enough space to pump. Your cat's not getting enough oxygen."

I felt the blood drain out of my face, and I swallowed hard.

"In this condition, he probably doesn't have more than a few days to live. Two weeks at the most, I guess." He paused. "It's up to you if you want to bring him home for his last days, but know that he'll be in constant pain if you do."

My thoughts fit together into the irrevocable truth of our condition in this world, which I strived so hard to deny every day. As fiercely as I loved Avalon, I pledged I would never let anything bad happen to him and that we would be together forever. I had done everything I could to keep that promise, yet, ultimately, I had failed. In that moment, I knew such a promise was by its nature impossible to keep. I could try to protect Avalon, but I couldn't keep life from happening to him. Just as everyone else, Avalon was vulnerable to all the afflictions and misfortunes of this world. And with that realization came the knowledge of the pain Avalon was in now and of the hard decision I had to make.

"I don't want him to suffer," I said.

"The valium has already made him unconscious. If I give him the injection now, he won't realize what's happening."

"Avalon means everything to her," Dominique said. "He's the only thing she has."

"I'm so sorry," the vet answered. "I'm going to leave the two of you alone for a while so you can say goodbye properly."

I bent over Avalon and kissed his mouth, his head, his back, his paws. I told him how much I loved him, how he had always been the one for me, how happy he had made me, and how I wouldn't trade one minute of one day with him for anything in the world.

Though his eyes were open, he didn't react. They looked vacant as if he was already gone, and in some way he was. I wasn't sure if he heard me, but it didn't really matter, because these were the words I had told him every single day for years. Avalon knew what I felt for him.

After a while, I can't say if it was ten minutes or half an hour, Dominique asked me if I was ready, if she could call the vet. I didn't answer. I would never be ready.

She hesitated for a second then left the room to call him.

Less than an hour after we arrived at the veterinary hospital, Avalon died peacefully in my arms while I told him how much I loved him. He didn't seem to have suffered from his passing.

"Is he gone?" I asked after a minute.

The vet nodded.

***

In the evening, I wrote on Avalon's blog, "Never had I expected to love a cat this much. He was the one who taught me about love, about what it meant to love unselfishly. Our relationship was so fusional we could never be more than a few hours without each other. How I am supposed to live the rest of my life without him, I really don't know. With Avalon, I lost my companion, my soulmate, the one great love of my life. Our relationship was the kind that transcended time and space and, I'm sure, will even transcend death. I will love you forever, Avalon."

EPILOGUE

I'm sitting on the balcony of my new apartment, writing the last paragraphs of this book. It's barely light out, despite the clock hitting 8:00 in the morning. It's quiet. The only sounds are the soft early-morning chirping of birds and, once in a while, the passing of a nearby train. The tiles beneath my feet haven't yet warmed from the sunrise.

Gilles and I now live on the same street where Avalon spent his kittenhood. From where I sit, if I look behind the gardens and trees, I can spot a glimpse of where I met my soul cat. And every time I pass the crossing of these two streets, I imagine him walking by, stopping in his tracks as if he recognized me, coming over to say hi, and never leaving my side again for the rest of his life.

And what a life it was.

By writing this book, I became aware of the impact he had on me, one that transcended the moments of love and laughter.

Many argue that my relationship with Avalon was unhealthy, but it was actually the opposite. We became emotionally stable beings because we had each other. We had both been our worst selves when we met, but we had bonded through an unwavering desire to be loved unconditionally and to love just as much in return. What we thought impossible, we had found with each other.

Today is exactly one year that Avalon passed, and even without his physical presence, he remains the driving force in my life. Avalon was a fixture, beside me in everything I did, and somehow that is still the case. His absence has pushed me to travel abundantly and to visit several international film festivals, including the famous Cannes film festival, something I would never have done before (although, I have to admit that when I arrived at one of the world's most beautiful beaches, I cried because its beauty wasn't even close to that of the cat I loved so much). He has inspired me to start my blog Traveling Cats, an online collection of my travel photos of cats, which has since become one of my biggest successes. He rekindled my friendship with Stephan, because we met again after many years so we could both say goodbye to Avalon and we are now on good terms again. And, finally, writing this book helped me understand the causes of my insecurities and come to terms with them.

But a piece of me is missing. Wherever Avalon is now, he has taken that part with him--the part that was my purpose in life to make him happy and imbued me with a strong sense of belonging.

When we adopt a pet in our twenties, we don't have a clear concept of death. We know pets will abandon us someday, but what is "someday"? Fifteen or twenty years? That equals a lifetime for a twenty-year old. And so we love with full abandon because we expect our pet will last a lifetime. And when life doesn't turn out as planned, we love the pet even more because it's all we have. It becomes our map and globe, our route and compass. We become each other's world.

By writing Avalon's memoir, I have come up against a wall many times. It was particularly hard to talk about my past and my failures. I wish I could have been much stronger and more of a leading lady, but I had to be honest about my pains to explain why Avalon and I were so attached to one another. Only when I talked about myself in direct conjunction with Avalon, was I able to feel a certain acceptance. Of course, that was because the only times I found myself likeable was when I saw myself through Avalon's eyes.

I also lacked the words to describe how precious Avalon was to me. Like when you talk about a movie that touched you deeply or a vacation that changed your life, nothing you say will ever convey the exact feeling it gave you. I had to accept that, although I have done my best to paint this portrait of him, I am incapable of doing him justice. The ineffable cannot be described.

Gilles advised me to downgrade my fusional bond with Avalon for fear that its magnitude would put people off. But that fierce intensity, that obsession with each other, is what colored our relationship, what made it so pure and tender. I owe it to Avalon to portray our love the way it was. After all, I wrote this book to honor him, to keep his beautiful spirit alive. Avalon deserves so much more than just one lifetime and this memoir was an attempt to grant him that alternate existence.

I started this book with the hope that the more people would read his story, the more something of his spirit would linger on. Now that it's finished, I understand that what I truly wanted was to relive our life together through my writing. It doesn't matter if a million people fall in love with Avalon, because all their awe combined wouldn't even match mine.

I wanted to eternalize Avalon, make him important to the world, but we were each other's world, and I am so incredibly grateful for the little eternity that was accorded to us.

Made in United States
Orlando, FL
20 September 2023

37121740R00074